Country Medallion

SAMPLER

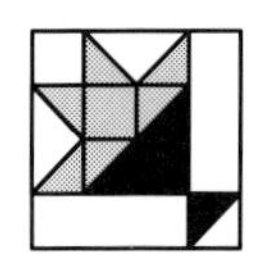

Carol Doak

Acknowledgments

My heartfelt thanks and appreciation are extended to:

My students, who make teaching the art of quiltmaking a real joy.

My quilting friends, for their unwavering encouragement and support.

Doreen Burbank, for sharing her appreciation for the quick and easy approach to the art of quiltmaking.

My husband, Alan, for being so supportive of all my quilting endeavors.

Barbara Weiland, for always being there with her friendly encouragement and support.

Credits

Editor-in-Chief ....Barbara Weiland
Technical Editor ....Kerry I. Hoffman
Managing Editor ....Greg Sharp
Copy Editor ....Liz McGehee
Proofreader ....Tina Cook
Text and Cover Design ....Kay Green
Typesetting ....Julianna Reynolds
Photography ....Brent Kane
Illustration and Graphics .....Laurel Strand

That Patchwork Place, Inc.
PO Box 118
Bothell, WA 98041-0118
USA

Printed in the United States of America
98 97 96 95 94 93   6 5 4 3 2 1

Doak, Carol.
Country medallion sampler / Carol Doak.
p. cm.
ISBN 1-56477-046-X :
1. Patchwork—Patterns. 2. Machine quilting—Patterns
I. Title.
TT835.D6 1993
746.9'7—dc20
93-32533
CIP

Contents

Introduction

When I began designing this quilt, I had several goals in mind. I like country-style quilts and love the dramatic statement that a medallion quilt makes. I wanted to create a quilt that would be easy for a beginning quilter to complete. So I assembled a collection of traditional patchwork blocks and created variations of them. The resulting quilt has large, open areas where you can showcase pretty quilting designs. Although the quilt looks intricate, it is easy to make.

I used the rotary cutter and rotary rulers to cut the pieces whenever possible. Even when templates were required, I used the rotary cutter to cut simple shapes. I also used quick and easy machine-piecing methods.

Tips, such as rounding template points to match up angled shapes, piecing perfect points, and matching seams, are included in the "General Instructions," below.

This Country Medallion Sampler quilt accomplishes all of my original goals. The bonus is that the variety of 9" block designs makes this quilt a good learning tool and great fun to make.

I hope that you learn some helpful techniques and have fun making your special quilt.

Sincerely,

Carol

General Instructions

This chapter includes a basic review of rotary-cutting techniques and piecing directions for the patchwork blocks. If you are a beginner, be sure to read through this information before starting your quilt. If you are more experienced, refer to this chapter for a brief refresher course on the various techniques included in the directions for the individual blocks.

Rotary-Cutting Basics

Most of the pieces for the blocks in the Country Medallion Sampler are rotary cut. Strip and piece dimensions given include 1/4"-wide seam allowances. Some blocks require templates, which begin on page 46. These also include the required seam allowances. Basic rotary-cutting directions follow. For more detailed information on rotary cutting, see *Shortcuts: A Concise Guide to Rotary Cutting* by Donna Lynn Thomas.

Equipment

For rotary cutting, you will need a rotary cutter, a rotary cutting mat, and one or more rotary-cutting rulers. These are made of a clear acrylic with measurements commonly marked in 1/8" and 1/4" increments. Some handy ruler shapes and sizes include 6", 12", and 16 1/2" squares; 6" and 8" Bias Square®; 3" x 18" ruler; 6" x 24" ruler (especially handy for cutting strips).

Rotary-cutting mats are available in several colors. I recommend using a dark-colored mat when cutting light-colored fabrics and a light-colored mat when cutting dark-colored fabrics. The contrast makes it easier to see the fabric edges.

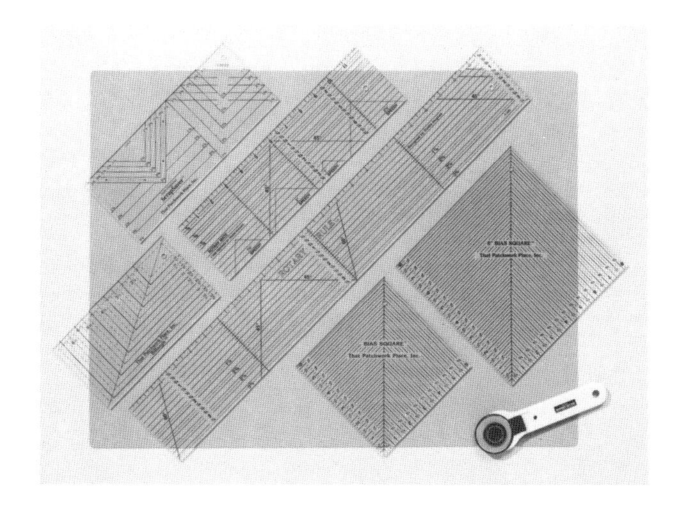

In some cases, you will be directed to glue (using a washable glue stick) a cutting template to a rotary ruler. To save time, cut all pieces requiring that template, rather than removing it from the ruler only to find that you must replace it later to cut more pieces. Simply scan the cutting list for that block, cut from the appropriate fabrics, label with the piece number, and set aside to use later.

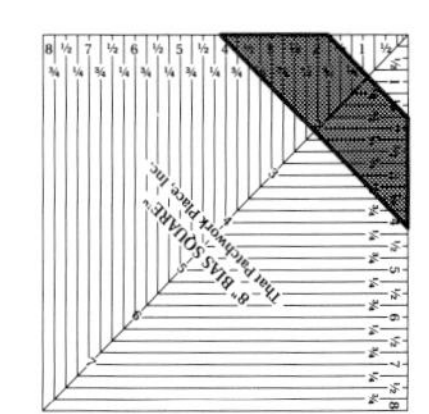

Plastic template glued to ruler.

Tip

To keep a rotary ruler from slipping out of place while you cut, apply small tabs of sandpaper at the corners on the underside of the ruler.

Preparing to Rotary Cut

Before cutting the pieces for the blocks in your quilt, take the time to wash your fabrics to eliminate shrinkage. Press the laundered fabrics to remove wrinkles.

To cut squares and rectangles from scraps of fabric:

1. Layer up to six scraps of fabric large enough to accommodate the piece you need. Be sure to align the lengthwise and crosswise grains as much as possible.
2. Position the Bias Square on a corner of the fabric stack so that the outside edges are along the straight of grain.
3. Make two cuts along the edges of the ruler to separate the squares or rectangles from the rest of the fabric scraps.
4. Carefully turn the fabric layers around (or turn the mat) and position the Bias Square at the desired cutting size. Make the final two cuts to complete the fabric squares or rectangles.

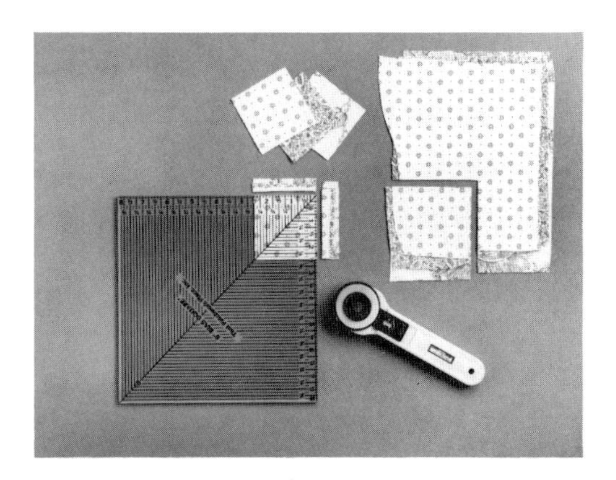

Shapes such as squares, triangles, rectangles, and diamonds may be rotary cut from fabric strips. This is a speedy way to cut the required pieces for your quilt. Most strips are cut across the fabric width, but some must be cut on the bias (when making bias squares).

To cut strips for patchwork pieces:

1. Fold the fabric in half with selvages matching.
2. Position the fabric on the cutting mat with the fold closest to you and the uneven edges to the left. (Reverse these directions if you are left-handed.)
3. Line up one edge of an 8" square ruler with the fold of the fabric. Position a 6" x 24" ruler to the left of the square and remove the square.
4. Make a clean cut across the width of the fabric, using a rotary cutter to cut along the right-hand edge of the ruler. Be careful not to let the ruler slip out of position as you cut away from yourself, using firm, downward pressure.

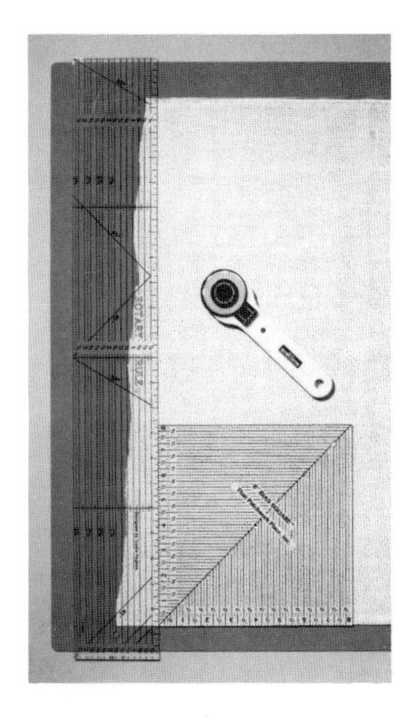

5. Cut strips of fabric, aligning the clean cut edge of the fabric with the ruler markings at the desired width.

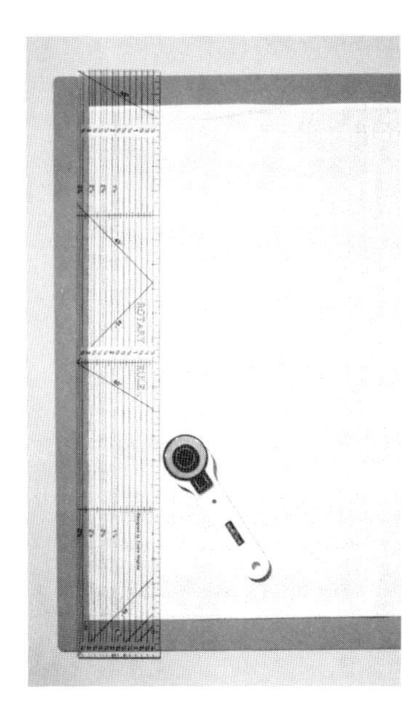

Cutting Squares and Rectangles

Several squares or rectangles can be cut from a strip of fabric. The outside edges of each piece cut from the strip are on the straight of grain.

To cut 3" squares:

1. Cut a 3"-wide strip across the width of the fabric long enough to make the needed number of squares, lining up the 3" mark on the ruler with the clean-cut edge of the fabric.

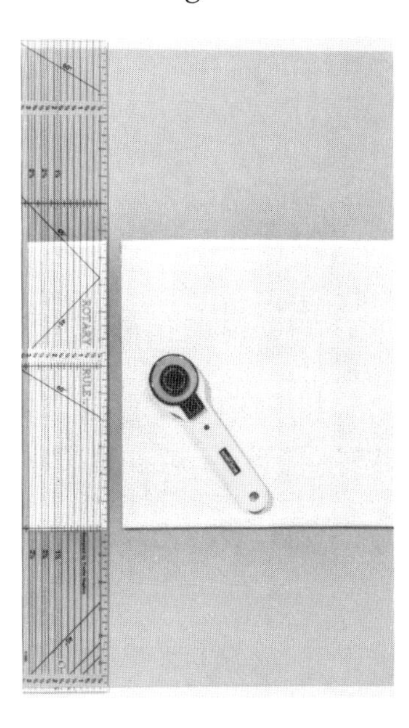

2. Turn the strip, line up the 3" mark on the ruler with the short end of the strip, and cut a 3" square. Continue in this manner, cutting the number of squares required for the block as directed in the cutting instructions.

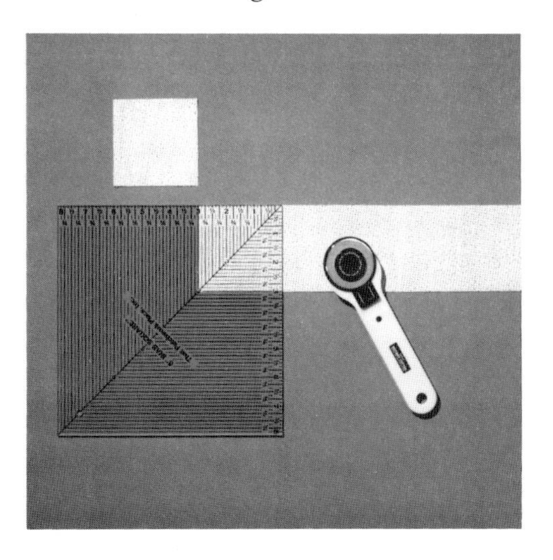

3. Squares and rectangles can be cut two at a time when the 3" strip is cut across the folded width of the fabric. Make sure that one of the horizontal lines on the ruler lines up with the folded edge of the fabric.

To cut rectangles from strips:

1. Make a clean cut as directed above, then cut a strip of the desired width.
2. Turn the strip on the rotary-cutting mat and line up the ruler at the size desired, along the short end of the strip. Cut. Repeat until you have the required number of rectangles.

Cutting Half-Square Triangles

Many patchwork designs include half-square triangle units—squares made of two right-angle triangles. To cut individual half-square triangles, first cut squares and then cut them on the diagonal. To allow for the seam allowance needed to join two half-square triangles into a square, you must add ⅞" to the desired finished size.

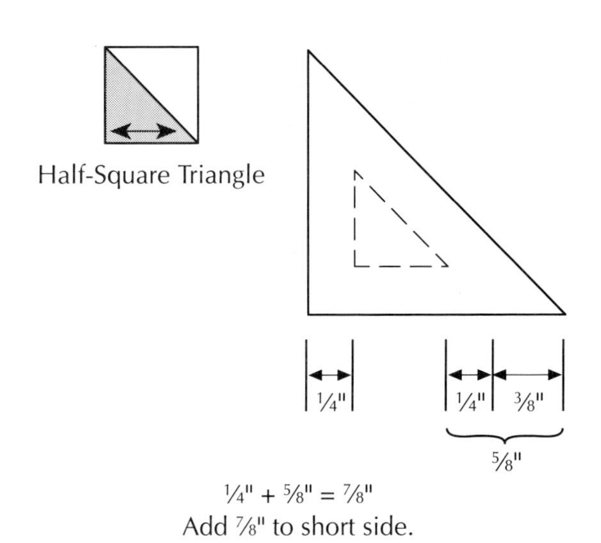

For example, if you want a 2" finished half-square triangle unit, cut strips 2⅞" wide and long enough to allow for the number of squares needed. Then crosscut the strips into 2⅞" squares; cut each square in half on the diagonal.

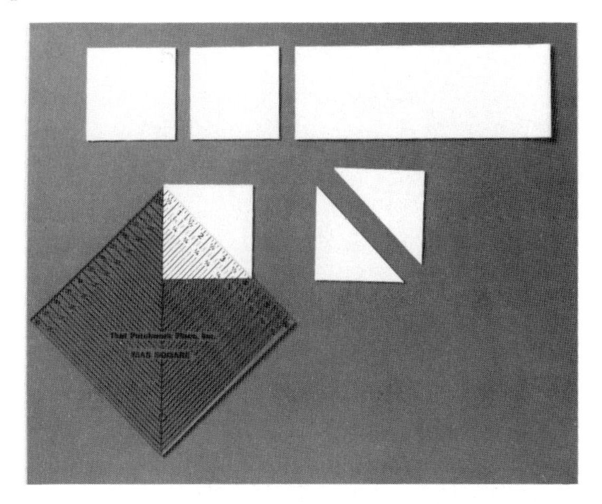

Making Bias Squares

You can also cut half-square triangle units (two triangles already sewn together through the center) from bias strips that have been seamed together in sets of two or in multiple sets. These are often called bias squares.

To make bias squares:

1. Cut bias strips from the required fabrics, cutting them ½" wider than the required finished square to allow for seam allowances. For example, if you need 2½" finished bias squares, cut 3"-wide bias strips.
2. Sew the strips together and press the seam toward the darker fabric.
3. Use the Bias Square to cut the units from the seamed strips. Beginning at the lower end of the strip-pieced unit, position the diagonal line of the Bias Square on the seam and cut two sides of the square the desired size.

Note: It's a good idea to cut the square 2–3 threads larger than the measurements given in the block pattern. Then trim it to size in step 4.

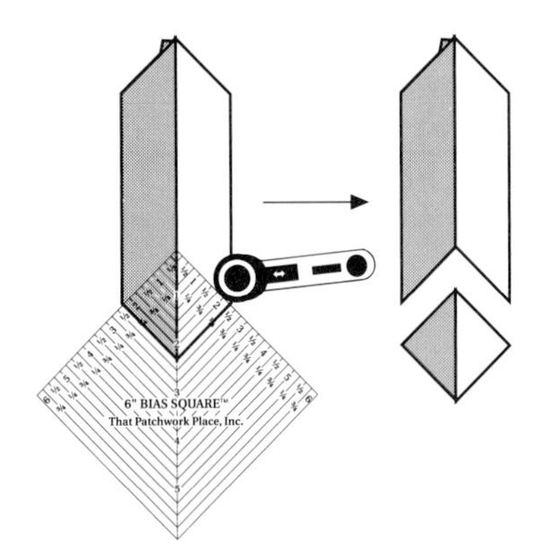

4. Turn the Bias Square 180° and cut the opposite sides of the square. Continue cutting bias squares in the same manner until you have the required number.

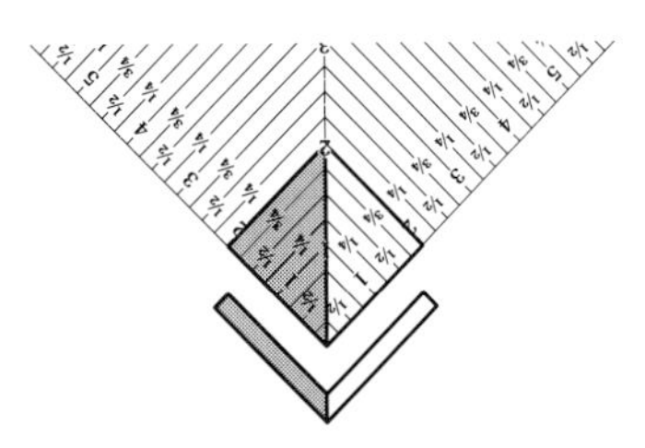

To make bias squares from multiple strip units:

1. Cut a 12" square from each of the fabrics required for the bias squares.
2. Place the 2 squares right sides together and make a diagonal cut through the center. Then cut bias strips of the required width from the resulting pieces.

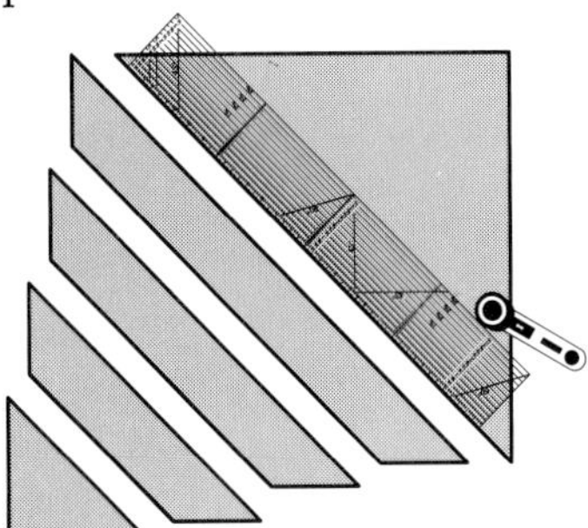

3. Join the strips in pairs and then join the strip pairs so the bottom points are even as shown.

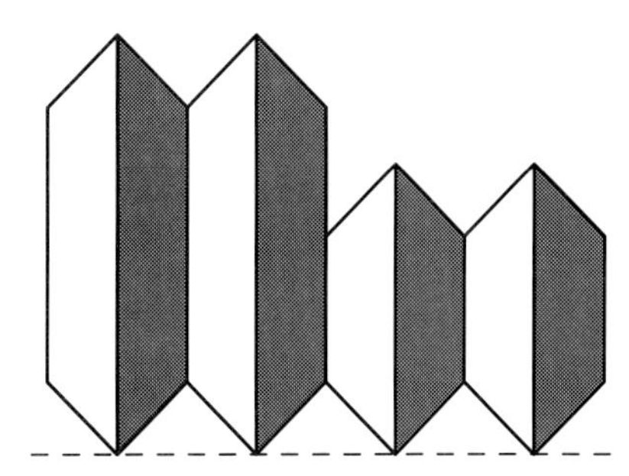

Bottom points even

4. Cut bias squares from the multiple strip units in the order shown below.

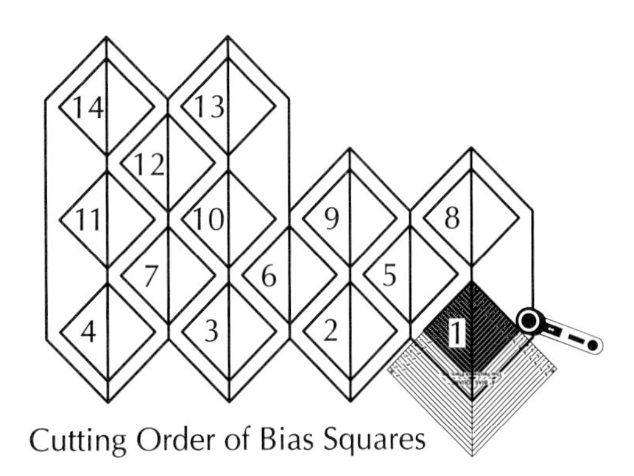

Cutting Order of Bias Squares

Cutting Quarter-Square Triangles

Many patchwork blocks require quarter-square triangles that have the straight of grain along the longest side. For four quarter-square triangles, cut a square that is $1\frac{1}{4}$" larger than the finished long side of the triangle. Then cut the square once diagonally and without moving the resulting pieces, cut diagonally in the other direction.

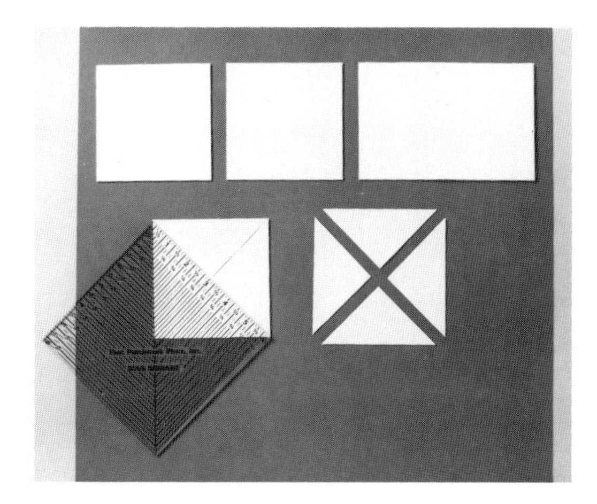

Making and Using Templates

If you have pieces that cannot be rotary cut from strips or simple geometric shapes, you will need to use a template for cutting. There are two ways to make and use templates. You may cut the required shape from template plastic, trace around it on the fabric, and cut it out, or attach the template to a rotary ruler to use as a cutting guide. Then you can cut the shape from a strip of the appropriate width, using the shape on the ruler as a guide.

Traditional Templates

Traditional templates are particularly appropriate when the shape is irregular or the cut measurement is in increments of less than $\frac{1}{8}$". Most rotary rulers are not marked in increments smaller than $\frac{1}{8}$", but some pieces in this quilt require measurements in $\frac{1}{16}$" increments. If your ruler is not marked in $\frac{1}{16}$" increments, measure halfway between two $\frac{1}{8}$" markings.

To make and use traditional templates:

1. Place opaque plastic template material on the template drawing and trace with a pencil and ruler along the outside edge. Mark the straight-grain arrow and the letter notation on the template. Also mark the dashed seam line when the template will be used to cut pieces from presewn strips, such as Templates I and K. The marked side of the template is the right side.
2. Cut out the shape on the marked line.
3. Place the template *wrong side up on the wrong side of the fabric* and mark the shape onto the fabric with a sharp pencil. If you also need reverse shapes, place the template right side up on the wrong side of the fabric and mark.

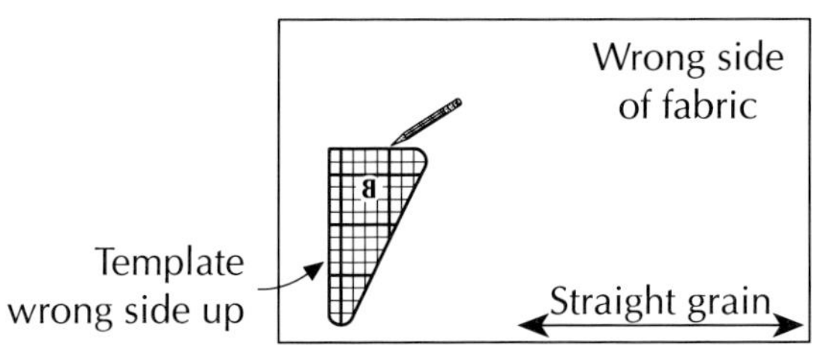

Hold pencil point at an angle to keep it sharp and prevent fabric drag.

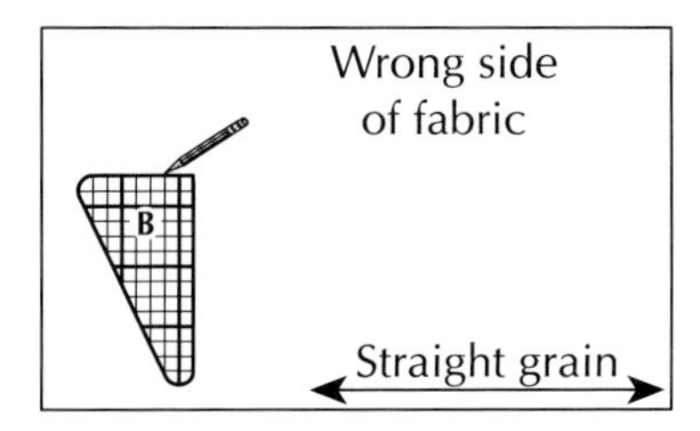

Reversed Template

4. Remove the template and using a rotary cutter and ruler (or a scissors if you prefer), cut out the marked shape.

TIP

To cut multiple pieces of the same shape at the same time, layer all of the fabrics wrong side up. Mark the shape on the top layer and cut through all layers. Do not layer more than six pieces of fabric in one stack.

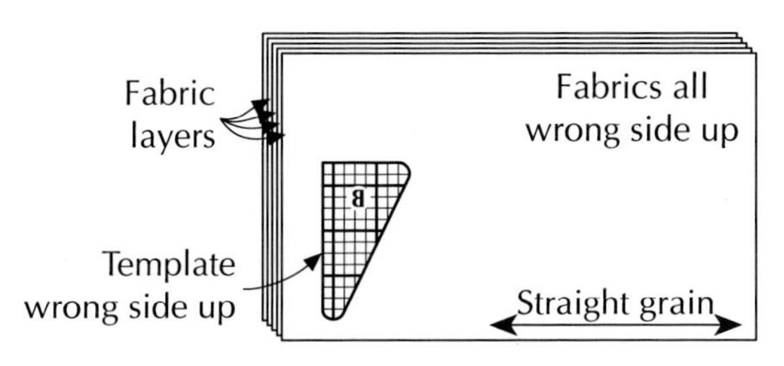

For sets of reverse shapes, layer the fabrics with right sides together.

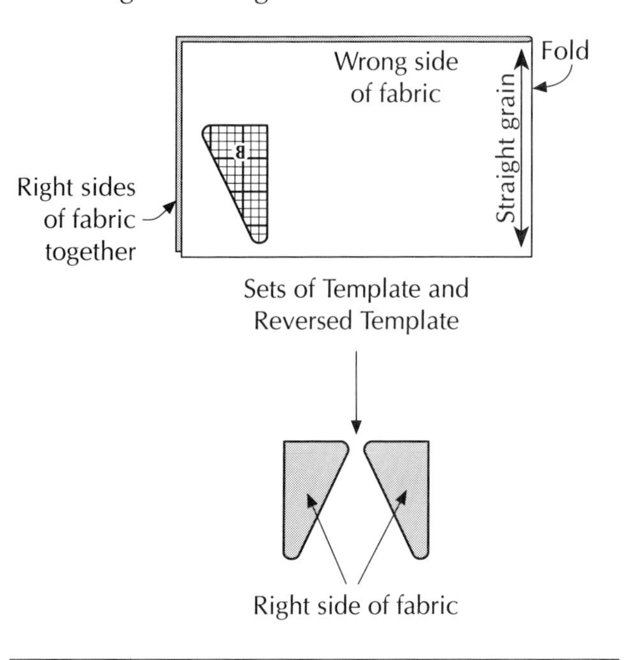

Sets of Template and Reversed Template

Note: For two of the blocks in the Country Medallion Sampler, I have provided templates with rounded points. Rounded points make it easier to match up the raw edges of some shapes, such as Templates A and B. My students have found this technique easier than trying to match seam intersections when pinning these pieces together for stitching.

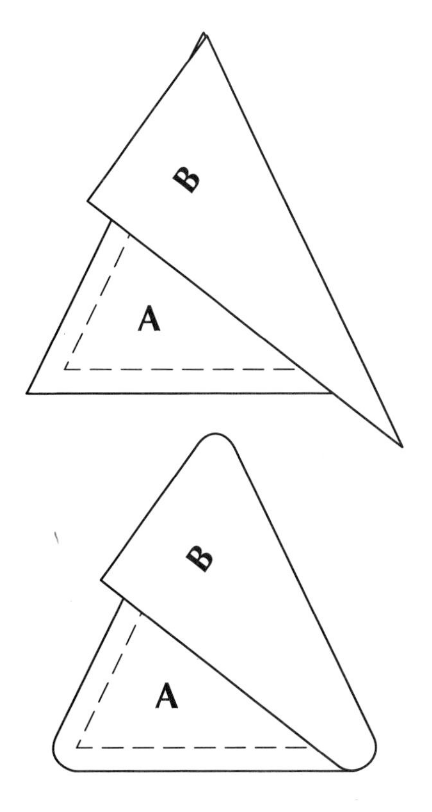

Cutting Guides

It is easy to cut geometric shapes, including shapes such as trapezoids and chevrons, with a plastic template glued to the underside of a rotary ruler.

To make and use a plastic template glued to a ruler:

1. Carefully trace the required template onto plastic, marking the grain-line arrow on the tracing.
2. Cut out the plastic template and use washable glue stick or removable transparent tape to secure the template face to the underside of the ruler. When positioning the template on the ruler and cutting the pieces, follow the directions below for the shape you are cutting.

Squares and Rectangles

Position these templates at the corner of the ruler to cut squares and rectangles.

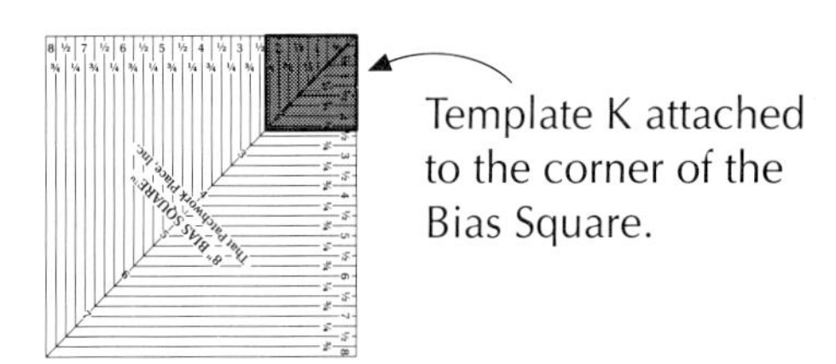

Half-Square and Quarter-Square Triangles

For half-square triangles, position the template at the corner of a ruler and place the long side of the template along the bias grain of the fabric. When several half-square triangles are needed, they can be cut from a bias strip as shown.

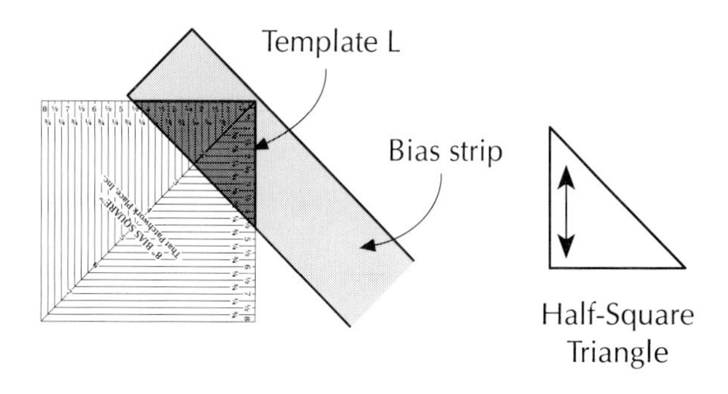

For quarter-square triangles, position the template at the corner of a ruler. Place the long side of the template along the straight grain of fabric. When you need several quarter-square templates, you can cut them from a straight-grain strip.

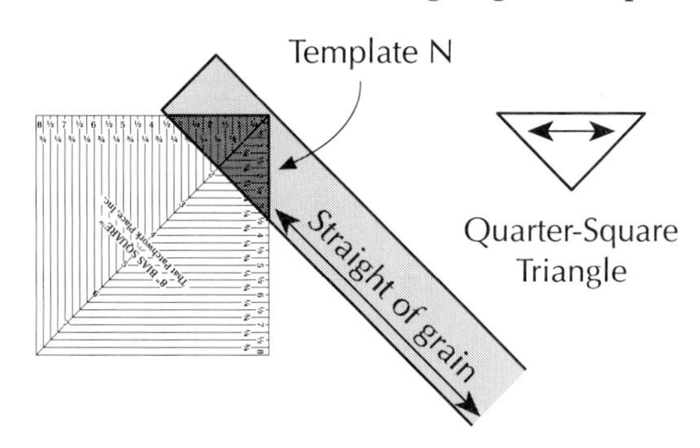

Trapezoids

It is easy to cut trapezoids using a Bias Square with a plastic template attached. First, you cut a right-angle triangle, called the "parent" triangle, then you cut away the right-angle corner.

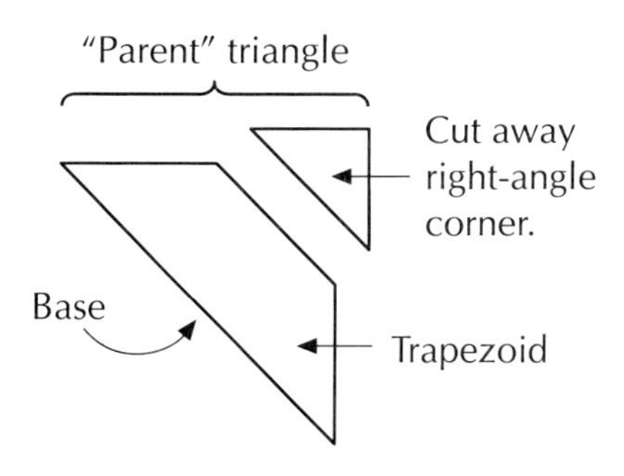

1. Make the required plastic template for the block.
2. Use glue stick or removable tape to secure the plastic template to the underside of the Bias Square. Position so the angled ends of the trapezoid are even with two adjacent sides of the Bias Square.

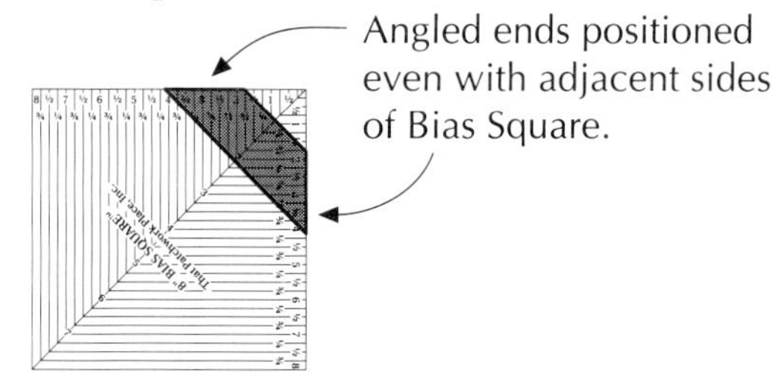

Attach template to underside of the Bias Square.

3. Cut a fabric strip in the required width by measuring the distance along the diagonal line from the corner of the Bias Square to the center of the base of the trapezoid. When the straight-grain arrow on the template is parallel to the base of the trapezoid as in Templates G and P, cut the strip on the straight of grain. When the straight-grain arrow is parallel to the angled end of the trapezoid as in Templates H and J, cut strips on the bias.

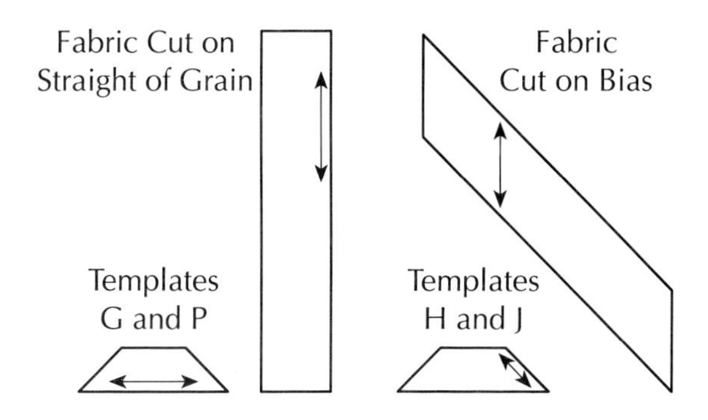

4. Place the Bias Square with plastic template on the fabric strip, with the base of the trapezoid even with bottom edge of the fabric strip. Cut out the "parent" triangle.

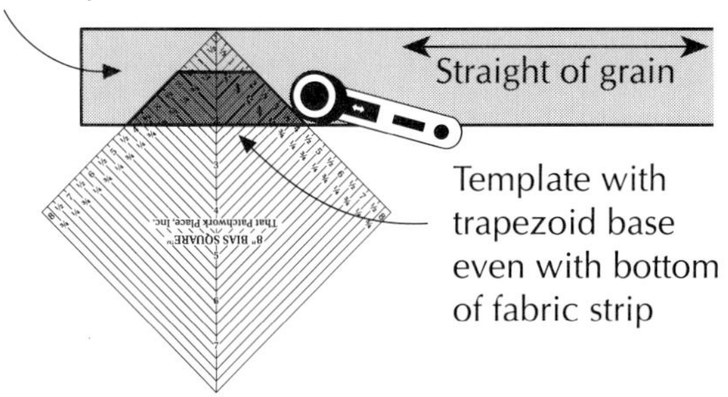

5. Remove the plastic template and reattach it, aligning the top edge of the trapezoid shape even with one edge of the Bias Square.

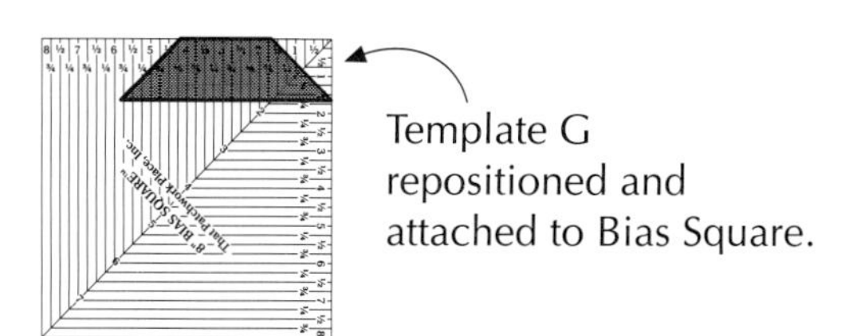

6. Place the Bias Square on the "parent" triangle, with the base of the trapezoid even with the long edge of the triangle. Cut along the edge of the Bias Square to remove the top corner of the triangle. Discard the triangle or save for another quilt project.

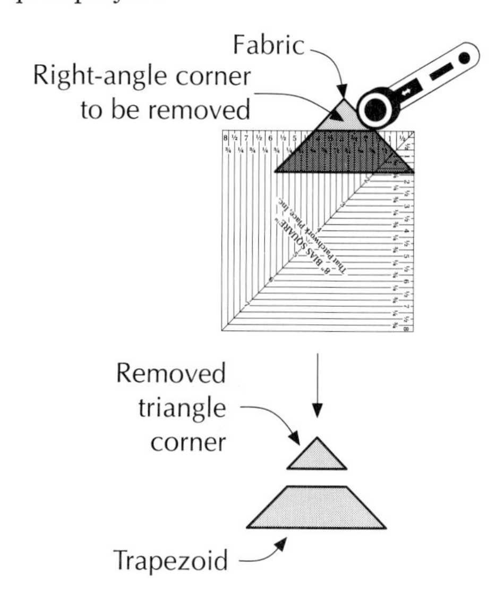

Chevrons

You may cut chevrons (also called parallelograms), using a ruler with a plastic template attached.

1. Make a plastic template, using the appropriate template (pages 46–48). In the following illustrations, Template C is shown as an example.
2. Position the straight-grain edges of the template, right side up, on the underside of the ruler at the lower right-hand corner.

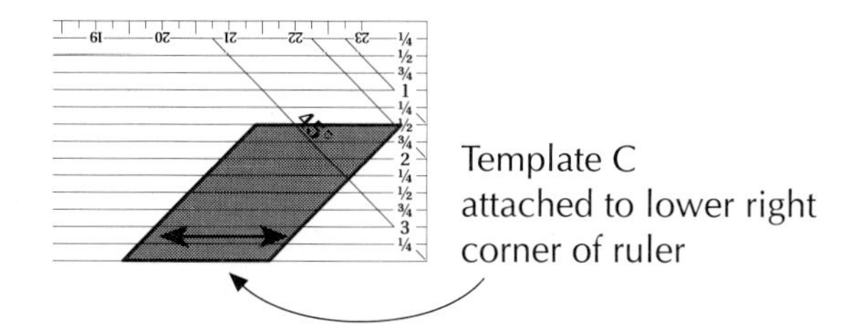

3. Prepare the fabric for rotary cutting by making a clean cut along the left-hand edge as shown on page 5.

4. Position the ruler with the end of the template even with the clean-cut edge of the fabric. Cut along the right-hand edge of the ruler to cut a strip of the correct width.

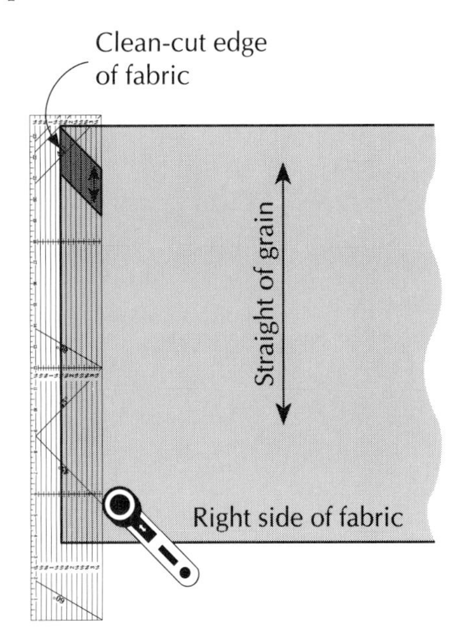

5. Remove the plastic template and reposition it on the ruler so the straight-grain arrow is at a 45° angle to the edge of the ruler.
6. Position the ruler so the top and bottom edges of the fabric strip are even with the edges of the chevron template and cut along the right-hand edge of the ruler.

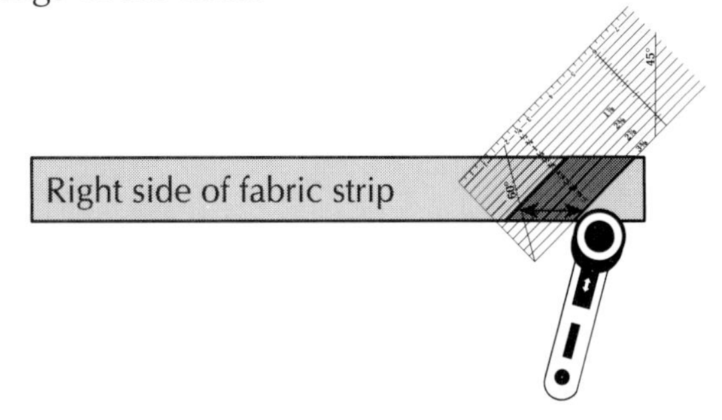

7. Pivot the cutting mat 180°, being careful not to disturb the fabric. Align the left edge of the plastic template with the cut end of the strip and cut along the right-hand edge of the ruler.

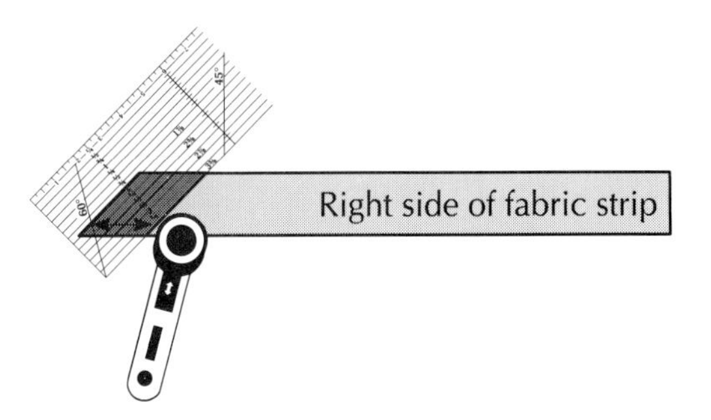

8. Continue cutting chevrons in this manner until you have the required number.

Note: If you need mirror-image chevron pieces, fold the fabric strip in half with wrong sides together. Cut as directed above, cutting two pieces at a time. The resulting pair will be mirror images of each other.

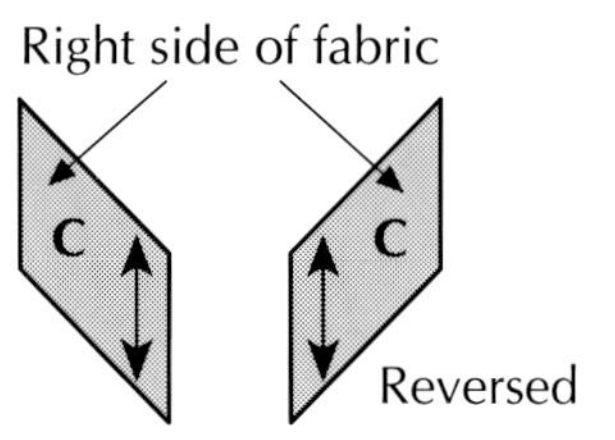

Machine Piecing

The Perfect Seam Allowance

To ensure successful piecing, you must sew an exact ¼"-wide seam allowance. To determine the exact ¼" location from your needle, place a rotary ruler under the presser foot and slowly drop the needle until it hits the ¼" line. Place several layers of masking tape along the edge of the ruler. If the location of ¼" from the needle falls under the presser foot and your zigzag sewing machine has the movable needle option, move the needle to the right and try again. If you do not have this option, cut a notch in the tape under the presser foot so it will not interfere with the feed dog.

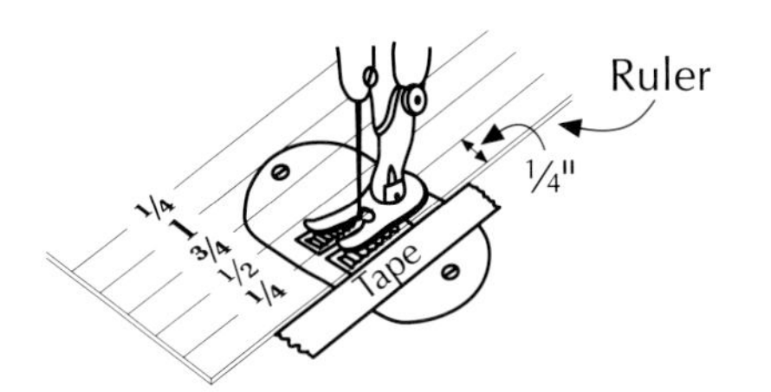

Test your masking-tape guide by cutting four strips of fabric, each 1½" x 3", and joining the long sides. The finished unit should measure 4½" wide exactly. If needed, repeat this process, adjusting the tape guide or the needle position until you have established an accurate ¼"-wide seam guide.

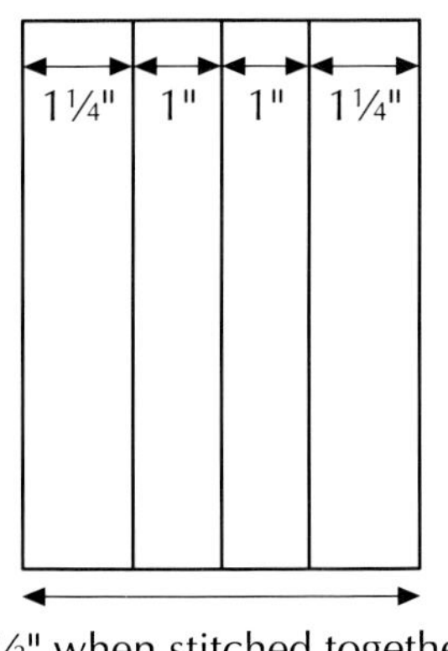

Machine-Piecing Tips

To save time and thread, chain sew one seam right after the other without cutting the thread. Stitch the seam, but do not lift the presser foot or clip the threads. Continue feeding in the next set of similar units as close as possible to the last set, until all of the units are sewn. Then clip the chain of units from the machine. You now have a long "string" of stitched units. Clip the units apart; press.

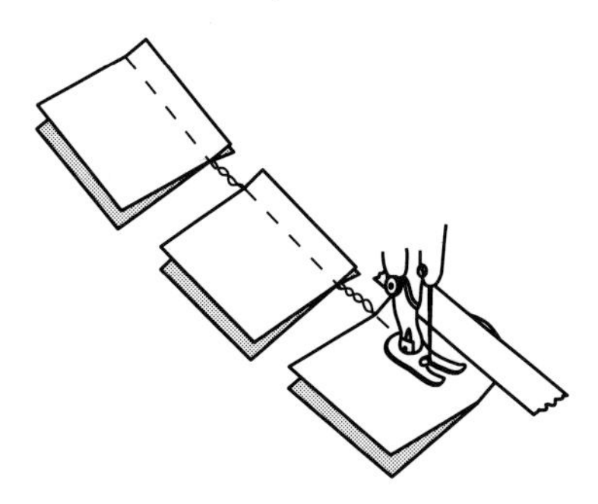

Trim away the "dog ears" on joined units so they will not interfere with the sewing process.

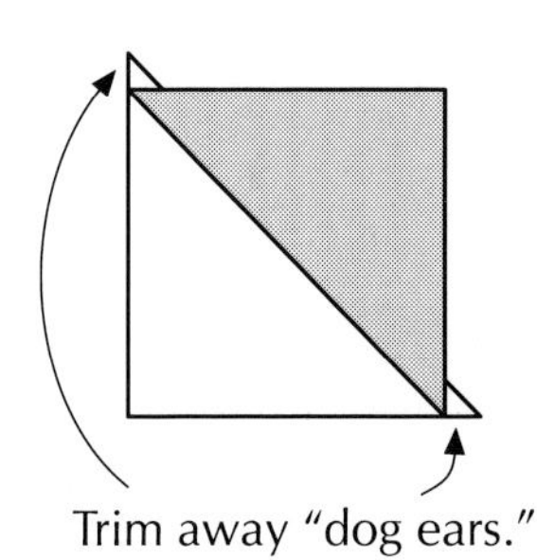

Trim away "dog ears."

Machine basting important seam intersections saves time and eliminates much frustration. With the sewing machine set on a long stitch, sew about 1" across the area of the intersection. When several matching places fall along a seam line, simply pull the piece to the next matching area and machine baste. If you are not pleased with the match, simply pull the thread out from the bobbin side of the mismatched seam and try again. When you are happy with all your intersections, sew the seam with the permanent stitching.

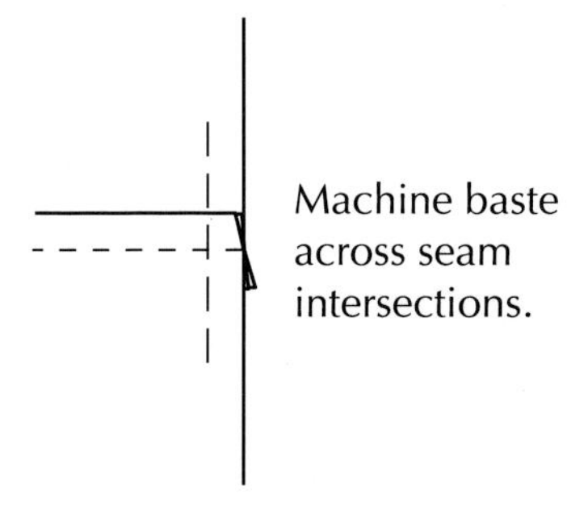

Machine baste across seam intersections.

When sewing across points, place the side with the points face up so you can cross the two previous seams at the top.

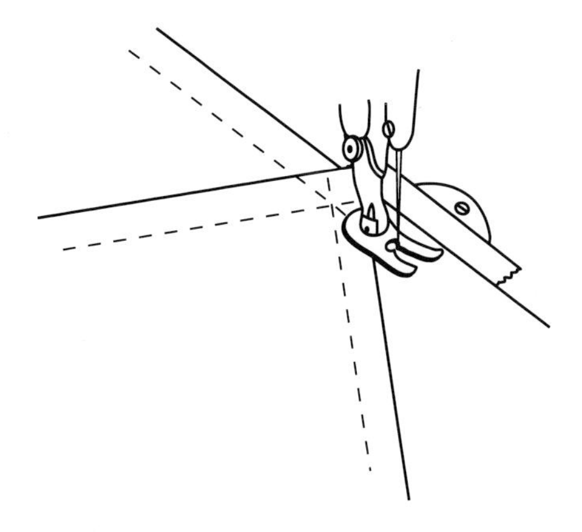

When joining two units that are seamed at the corner, begin sewing at the seamed corner for a good match.

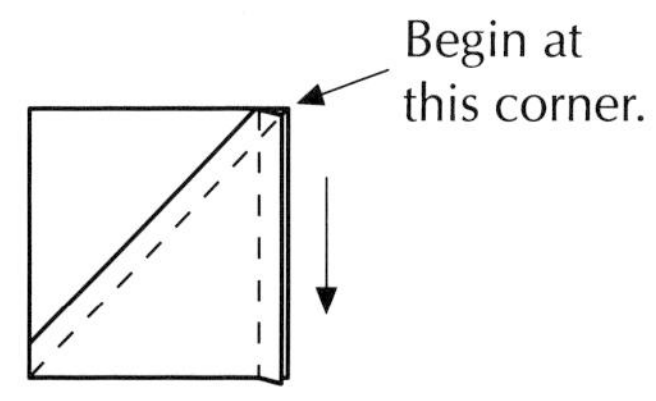

Pressing

When joining seams from two pieced units, butt seams at the intersections. To evenly distribute the seams and eliminate a bumpy intersection, press the seams in opposite directions so they will "snug up" to each other for a perfect match when you stitch across the intersection.

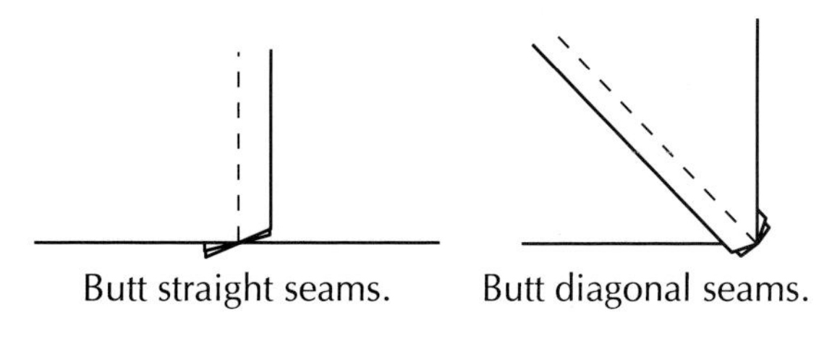

The patchwork pieces should be pressed, not ironed, with a dry iron set on the cotton setting. Let the weight of the iron do the work. Press the seam allowances away from points so the stitching lines are visible.

Quilt Plan

Finished Size: 86" x 86"
44 blocks, each 9" x 9"
5 blocks, each 18" x 18"
2"-wide inner border
5"-wide outer border, with 7" x 7" corner blocks

Country Medallion Sampler Blocks

I used blue, green, and pink fabrics with a light, medium, and dark value of each, set against a white background. However, you could easily substitute a light, medium, and dark value in three different colors of your choice.

A Color Key appears with the yardage requirements. I suggest you make your own color key, using small swatches of the fabrics you choose for your quilt.

Yardage and Fabric Key
Fabrics: 44"-wide

Yardage and Fabric Key

- White – 2½ yds.
- Dark blue – 2¼ yds.
- Medium blue – 2½ yds.
- Light blue – ⅔ yd.
- Dark green – ½ yd.
- Medium green – ⅓ yd.
- Light green – 1⅝ yds.
- Dark pink – ⅔ yd.
- Medium pink – ½ yd.
- Light pink – ½ yd.

8 yds. for backing

¾ yd. dark blue for bias binding*

*There should be enough dark blue fabric left over from the patchwork blocks to cut 2"-wide straight-grain binding. If you prefer to use bias binding, you will need an additional ¾ yard of the dark blue fabric.

Supplies

Rotary cutter, mat, and rulers. Some handy ruler sizes are:

6", 12", and 16½" squares

6" or 8" Bias Square

3" x 18" ruler

6" x 24" ruler (especially for cutting borders)

Masking tape

Opaque plastic template material

Washable glue stick

Cutting and Sewing the Patchwork Blocks

Fabric Key

- Dark blue
- Medium blue
- Light green
- White

The directions for each block are written with several visual clues. The Fabric Key box alerts you to the fabrics used. The Template Key box indicates any templates used and whether you will rotary cut them with the template attached to the ruler or mark them first with a pencil and then rotary cut.

Template Key

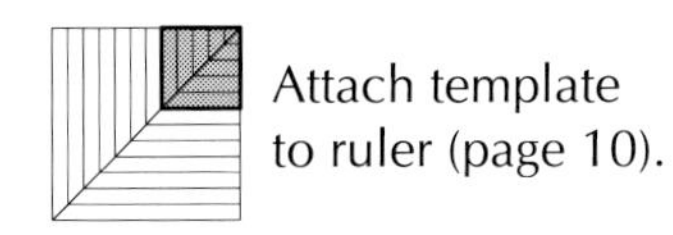

As you cut each group of fabric pieces, lay them out in block fashion, following the fabric placement illustration. The numbers indicate the exact placement for each piece.

When presewn units such as bias squares and seamed fabric strips are indicated, the method for making these follows the cutting list.

Follow the Piecing Sequence illustration to piece smaller units into larger units, units into rows or sections, and finally into the finished blocks.

Cutting the Border Strips

Cut and set aside the border strips before cutting into the yardage for the patchwork blocks so that you have strips of the required length. The cut lengths are actually a few inches longer than necessary. This is your insurance policy in the event the quilt grows during the construction process.

From the dark blue fabric, cut:
4 strips, each $2^1/_2$" x 75", for the inner border
4 squares, each $7^1/_2$" x $7^1/_2$", for the corner blocks

From the medium blue fabric, cut:
4 strips, each $5^1/_2$" x 75", for the outer border

Setting Blocks

Fabric Key

- Dark blue
- Medium blue
- Light green
- White

Blocks A, B, C, D, and E are setting blocks. You will combine them with the patchwork blocks to create the medallion-style quilt setting. Since they are made from larger pieces of fabric, it is wise to make the setting blocks now and set them aside. Refer to the Quilt Plan on page 14 for the location of each piece and the "General Instructions," beginning on page 4. Blocks A, B, C, and E are 9" finished, and Block D is 18" finished.

Cutting the Setting Blocks

From the dark blue fabric, cut:
#1—4 squares, each 9⅞" x 9⅞";
cut once diagonally for 8 half-square triangles

From the medium blue fabric, cut:
#2—8 squares, each 9⅞" x 9⅞";
cut once diagonally for 16 half-square triangles

From the light green fabric, cut:
#3—4 squares, each 9½" x 9½", for Block A

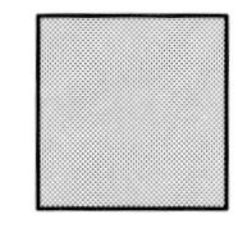

Block A

#4—4 squares, each 13¼" x 13¼"
#5—2 squares, each 10¼" x 10 ¼";
cut twice diagonally for 8 quarter-square triangles

From the white fabric, cut:
#6—8 squares, each 9⅞" x 9⅞";
cut once diagonally for 16 half-square triangles

#7—2 squares, each 10¼" x 10¼";
cut twice diagonally for 8 quarter-square triangles

Piecing the Setting Blocks

1. To assemble Block B, stitch the light green triangle (#5) to the white triangle (#7). Press the seam toward the light green triangle. Stitch this unit to the medium blue triangle (#2). Make 4.

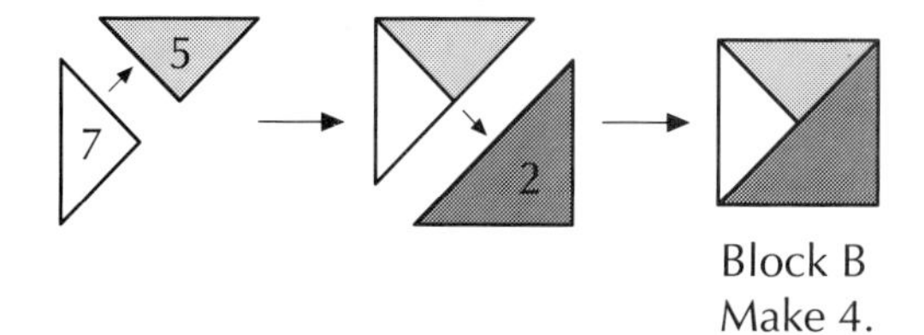

Block B
Make 4.

2. To assemble Block C, stitch the white triangle (#7) to the light green triangle (#5). Press the seam toward the light green triangle. Stitch this unit to the medium blue triangle (#2). Make 4.

Block C
Make 4.

3. To assemble Block D, stitch one white triangle (#6) to the light green square (#4). Next, stitch one medium blue triangle (#2) to the opposite side of the square. Press the seams toward the triangles. Repeat with the two remaining white and medium blue triangles to complete the block. Make 4.

4. To assemble Block E, stitch one white triangle (#6) to one dark blue triangle (#1). Press the seam toward the dark blue triangle. Make 8.

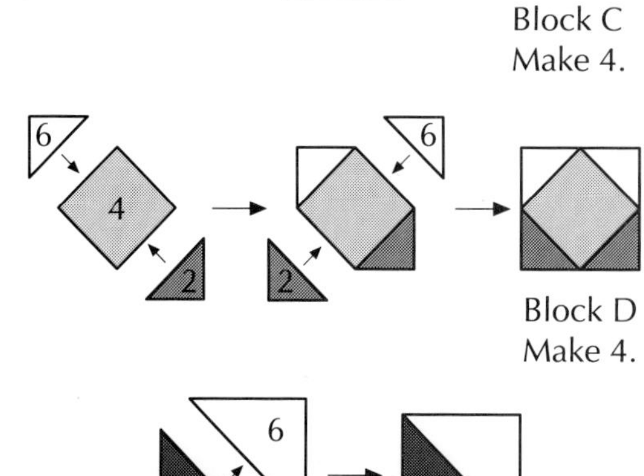

Block D
Make 4.

Block E
Make 8.

Ohio Star (Block F)

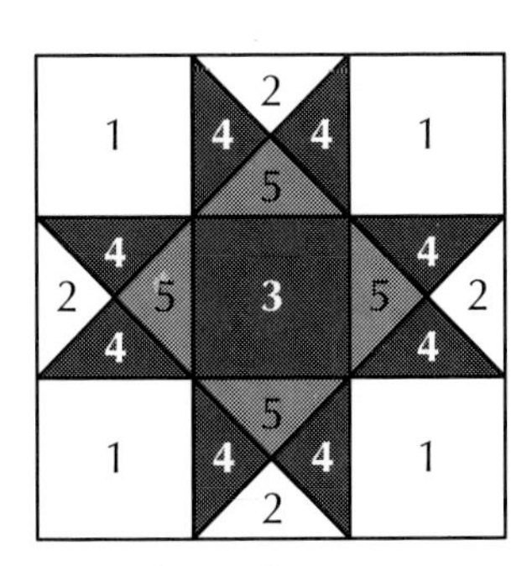

Fabric Placement
Ohio Star
Block F
Finished size: 9"

Fabric Key

- White
- Dark blue
- Medium blue

Cutting

From the white fabric, cut:
#1—4 squares, each $3^1/_2$" x $3^1/_2$"
#2—1 square, $4^1/_4$" x $4^1/_4$";
cut twice diagonally for 4 quarter-square triangles

From the dark blue fabric, cut:
#3—1 square, $3^1/_2$" x $3^1/_2$"
#4—2 squares, each $4^1/_4$" x $4^1/_4$";
cut twice diagonally for 8 quarter-square triangles

From the medium blue fabric, cut:
#5—1 square, $4^1/_4$" x $4^1/_4$";
cut twice diagonally for 4 quarter-square triangles

Assembly

Piecing Sequence

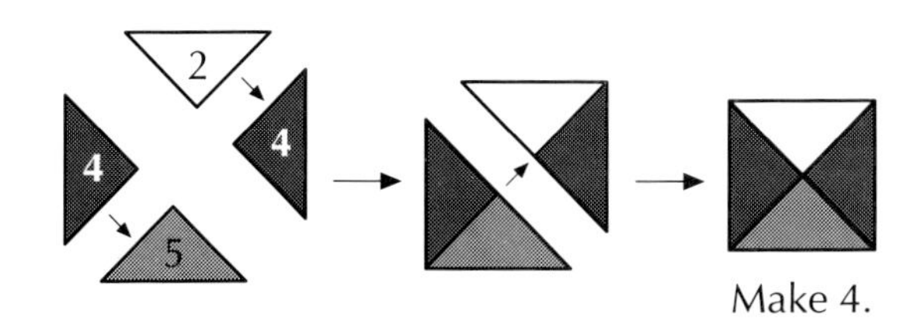

Block Assembly

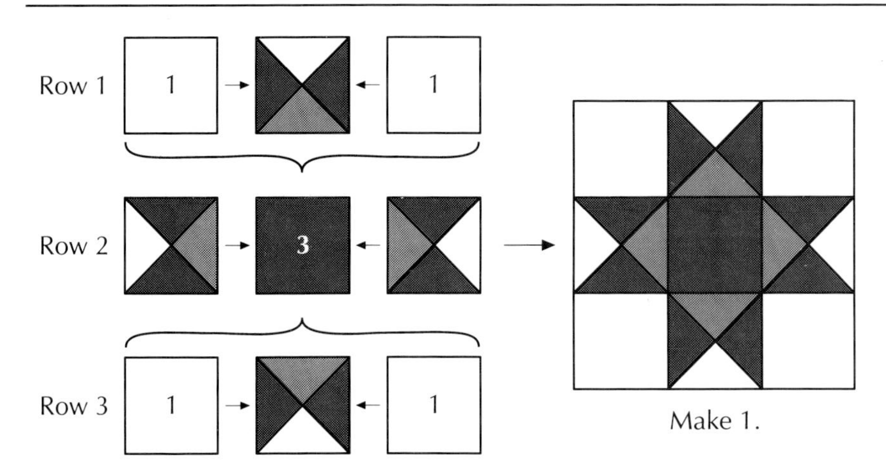

Cutting

From the white fabric, cut:
#1—4 squares, each 3½" x 3½"
#2—1 square, 4¼" x 4¼"; cut twice diagonally for 4 quarter-square triangles

From the dark blue fabric, cut:
#3—2 squares, each 3⅞" x 3⅞"; cut once diagonally for 4 half-square triangles

From the medium blue fabric, cut:
#4—1 square, 4¼" x 4¼"; cut twice diagonally for 4 quarter-square triangles

From the light blue fabric, cut:
#5—1 square, 3½" x 3½"

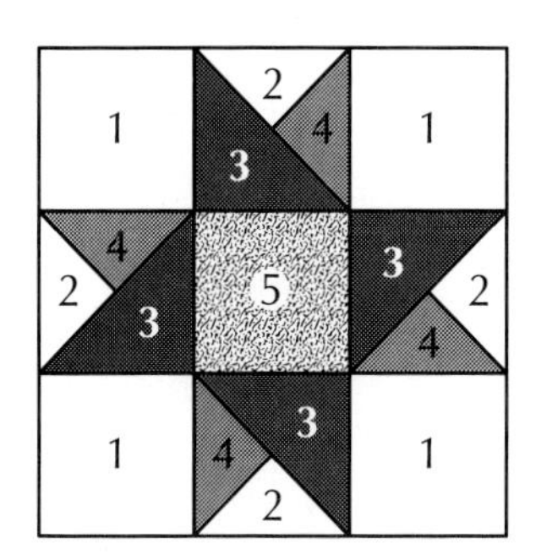

Fabric Placement
Twin Star
Block G
Finished size: 9"

Fabric Key

- White
- Dark blue
- Medium blue
- Light blue

Assembly

Piecing Sequence

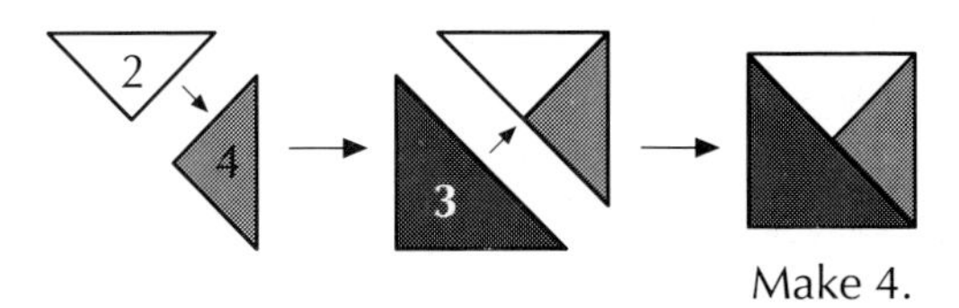

Make 4.

Block Assembly

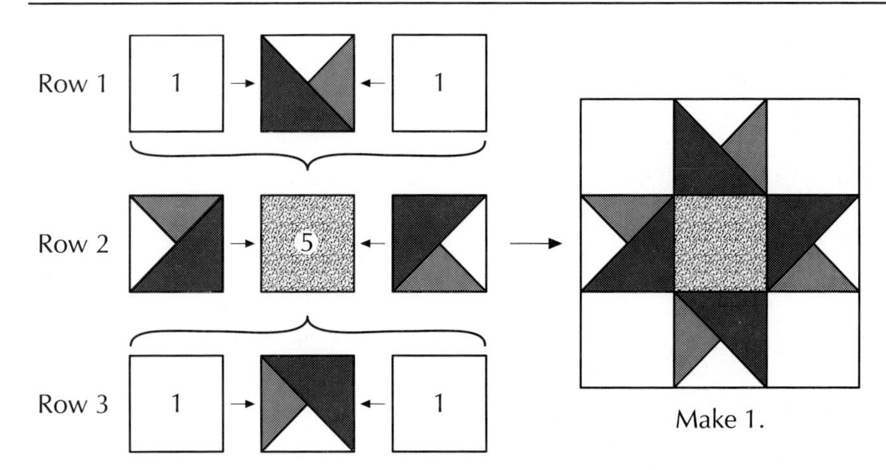

Make 1.

Card Basket Variation (Block H)

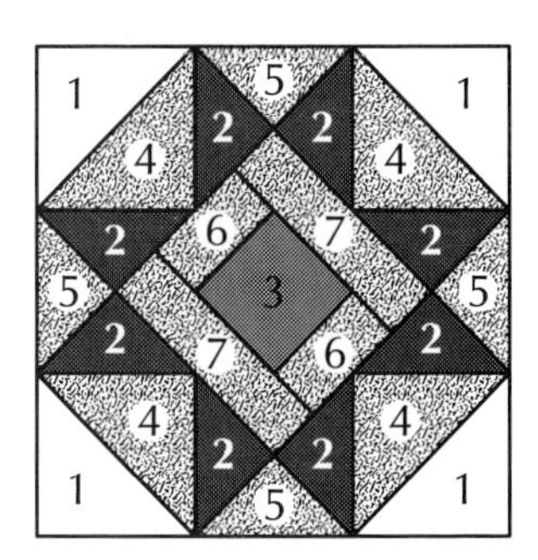

Fabric Placement
Card Basket Variation
Block H
Finished size: 9"

Fabric Key

- White
- Dark blue
- Medium blue
- Light blue

Cutting

From the white fabric, cut:
#1—2 squares, each 3⅞" x 3⅞"; cut once diagonally for 4 half-square triangles

From the dark blue fabric, cut:
#2—2 squares, each 4¼" x 4¼"; cut twice diagonally for 8 quarter-square triangles

From the medium blue fabric, cut:
#3—1 square, 2⅝" x 2⅝"

From the light blue fabric, cut:
#4—2 squares, each 3⅞" x 3⅞"; cut once diagonally for 4 half-square triangles
#5—1 square, 4¼" x 4¼"; cut twice diagonally for 4 quarter-square triangles
#6—2 rectangles, each 1 9/16" x 2⅝" *
#7—2 rectangles, each 1 9/16" x 4 11/16" *
*See "Traditional Templates" on page 8.

Assembly

Piecing Sequence

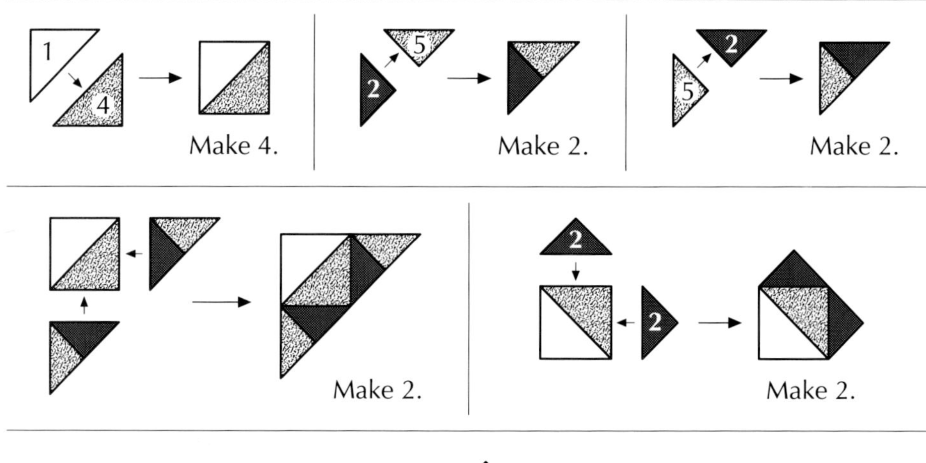

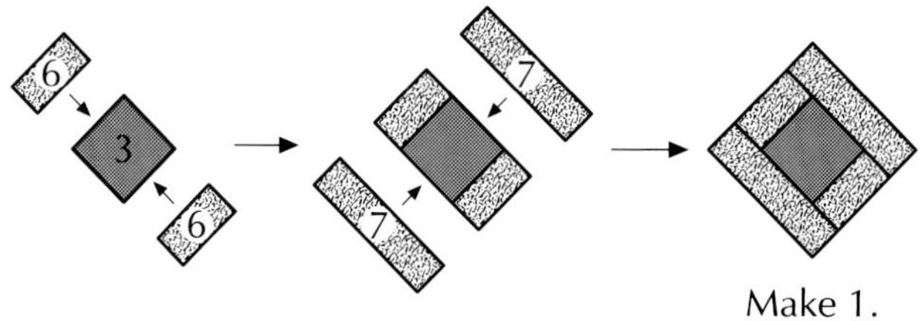

Block Assembly

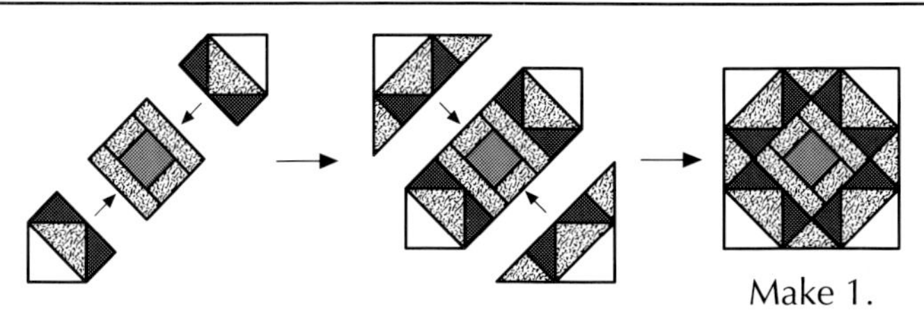

Cutting

From the white fabric, cut:
#1—8 squares, each 2" x 2"

From the dark blue fabric, cut:
#2—1 square, 4¼" x 4¼"; cut twice diagonally for 4 quarter-square triangles

From the medium blue fabric, cut:
#3—2 squares, each 4¼" x 4¼"; cut twice diagonally for 8 quarter-square triangles
#4—1 square, 3½" x 3½"

From the light blue fabric, cut:
#5—8 squares, each 2" x 2"
#6—1 square, 4¼" x 4¼"; cut twice diagonally for 4 quarter-square triangles

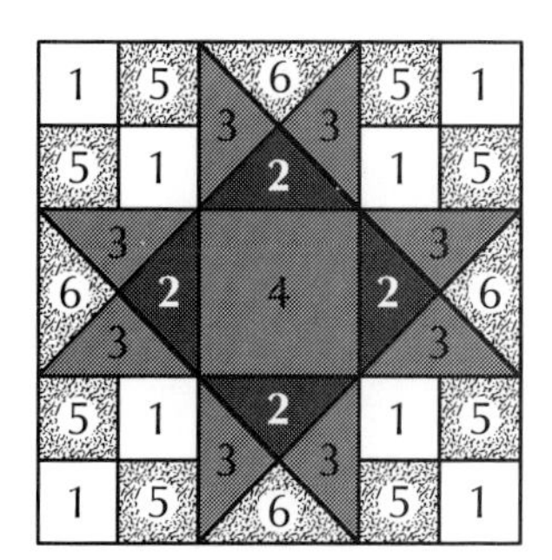

Fabric Placement
Country Star
Block I
Finished size: 9"

Fabric Key

- White
- Dark blue
- Medium blue
- Light blue

Assembly

Piecing Sequence

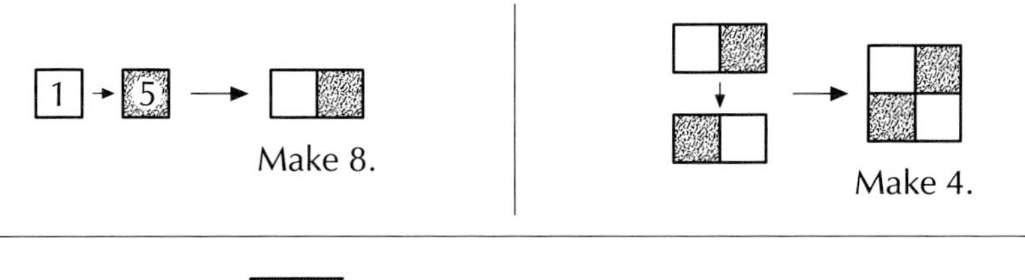

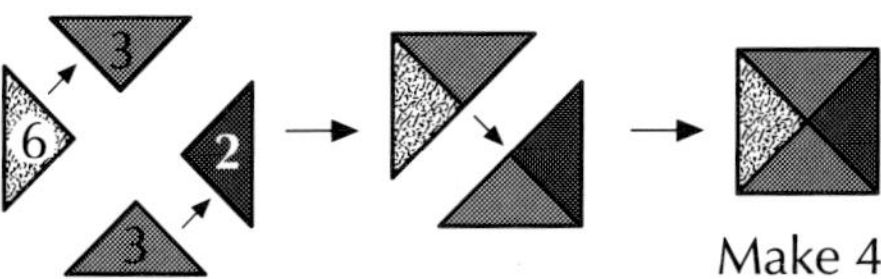

Block Assembly

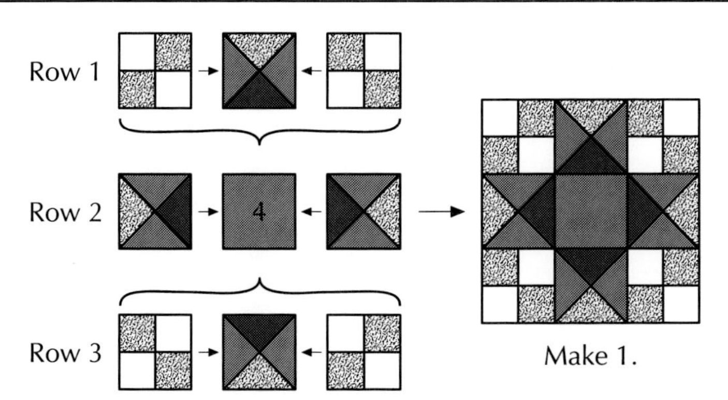

Bird of Paradise (Block J)

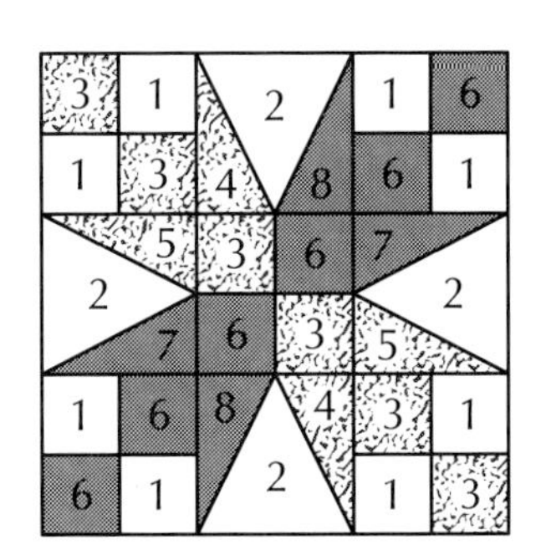

Fabric Placement
Bird of Paradise
Block J
Finished size: 9"

Fabric Key

Medium pink
Medium blue
White

Template Key

Trace around template.

Templates A, B, B reversed
Templates begin on page 46.

Cutting

From the white fabric, cut:
#1—8 squares, each 2" x 2"
#2—4 Template A

From the medium pink fabric, cut:
#3—6 squares, each 2" x 2"
#4—2 Template B
#5—2 Template B reversed

From the medium blue fabric, cut:
#6—6 squares, each 2" x 2"
#7—2 Template B
#8—2 Template B reversed

Assembly

Piecing Sequence

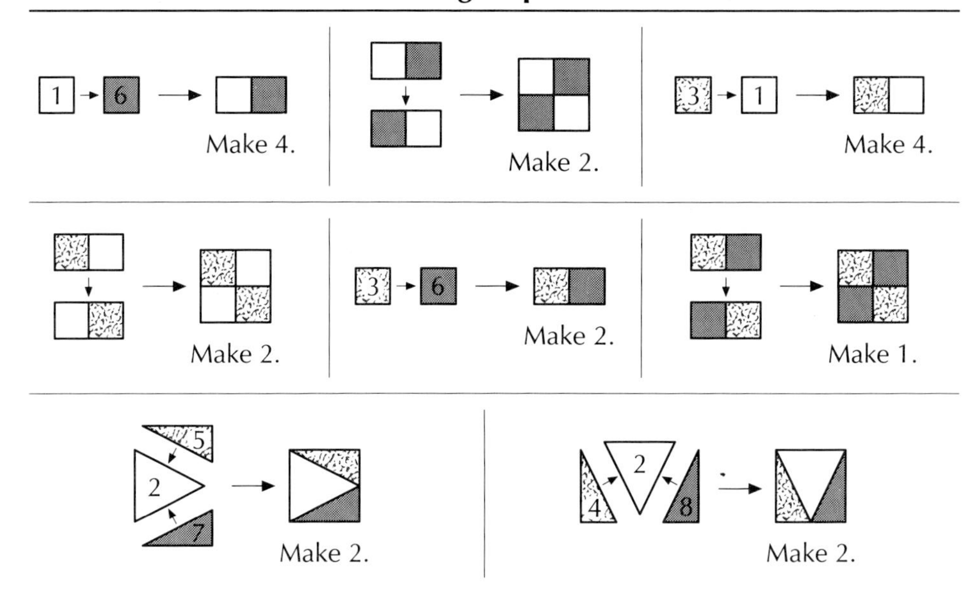

Block Assembly

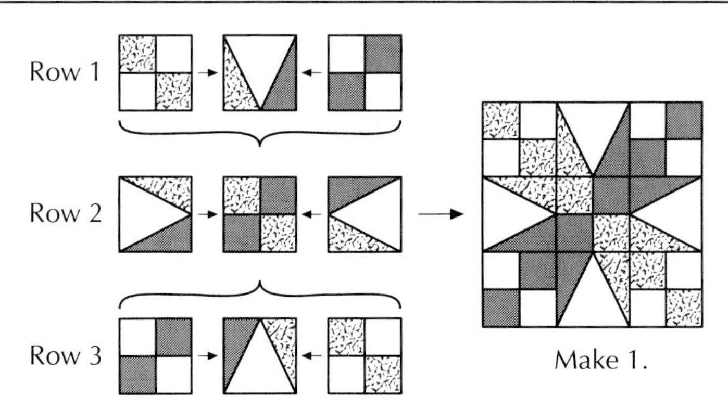

Cutting

From the white fabric, cut:
#1—4 squares, each 2" x 2"; cut once diagonally for 8 half-square triangles
#2—4 Template G

From the dark blue fabric, cut:
#3—4 Template G

From the medium blue fabric, cut:
#4—4 Template H

From the light blue fabric, cut:
#5—2 squares, each 2" x 2"; cut once diagonally for 4 half-square triangles

From the light green fabric, cut:
#6—2 squares, each $4^1/_4$" x $4^1/_4$"; cut once diagonally for 4 half-square triangles

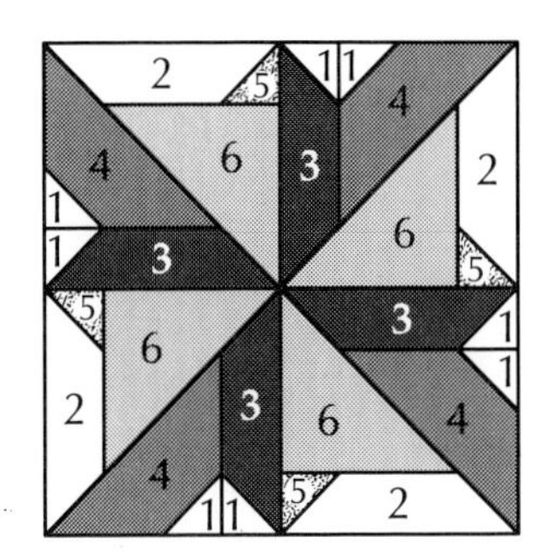

Fabric Placement
Whirling Star
Block K
Finished size: 9"

Fabric Key

- White
- Dark blue
- Medium blue
- Light blue
- Light green

Template Key

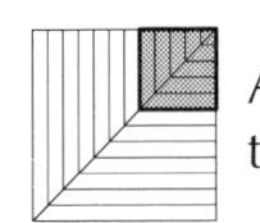

Attach template to ruler (page 10).

Templates G and H
Templates begin on page 46.

Assembly

Piecing Sequence

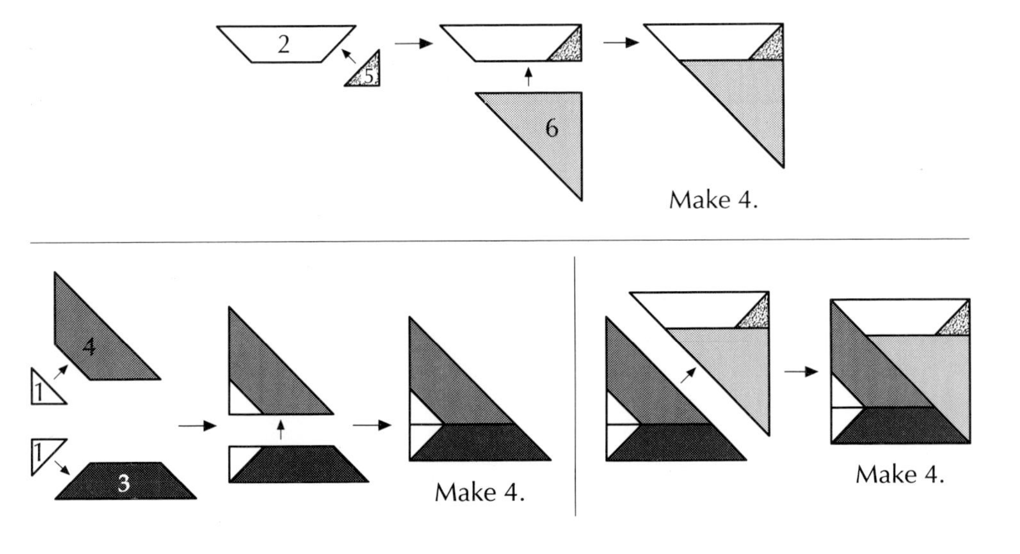

Block Assembly

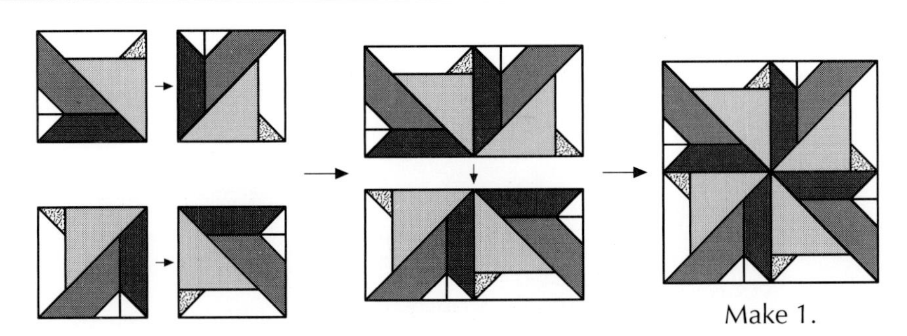

Wyoming Valley Variation (Block L)

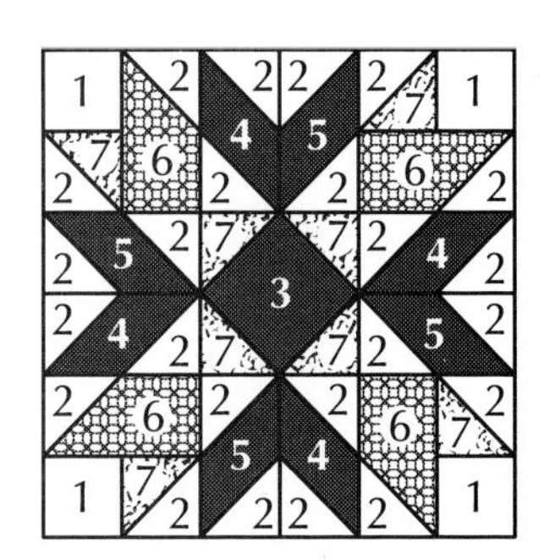

Fabric Placement
Wyoming Valley Variation
Block L
Finished size: 9"

Fabric Key

- White
- Dark blue
- Dark pink
- Medium pink

Template Key

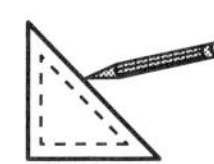

Trace around template.

Template D

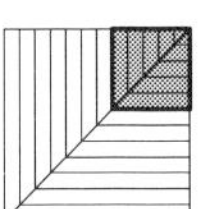

Attach template to ruler (page 10).

Templates C and C reversed
Templates begin on page 46.

Cutting

From the white fabric, cut:
#1—4 squares, each 2" x 2"
#2—12 squares, each 2⅞" x 2⅞"; cut once diagonally for 24 half-square triangles

From the dark blue fabric, cut:
#3—1 square, 2⅝" x 2⅝"
#4—4 Template C
#5—4 Template C reversed

From the dark pink fabric, cut:
#6—4 Template D

From the medium pink fabric, cut:
#7—4 squares, each 2⅞" x 2⅞"; cut once diagonally for 8 half-square triangles

Assembly

Piecing Sequence

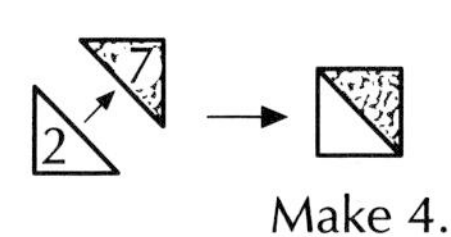

Make 4.

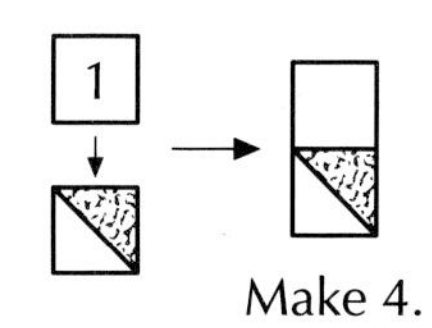

Make 4.

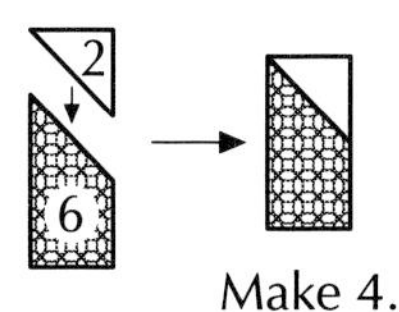

Make 4.

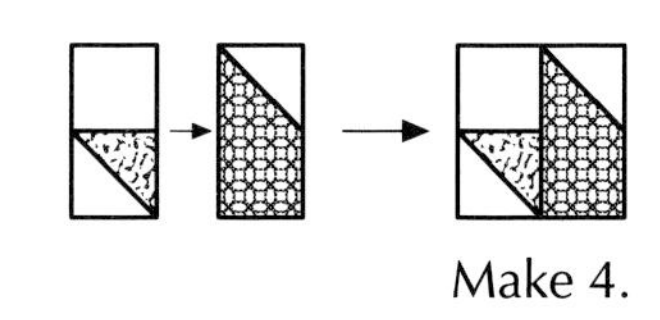

Make 4.

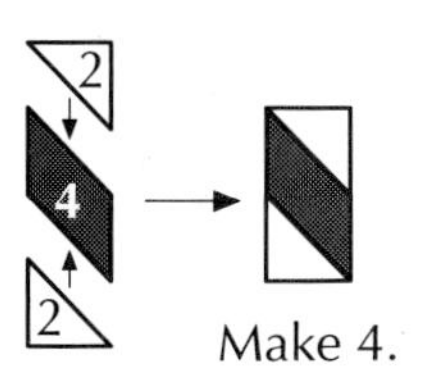

Make 4.

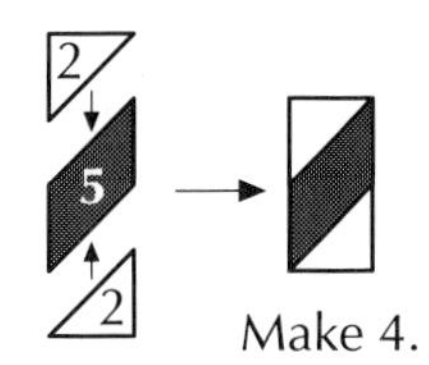

Make 4.

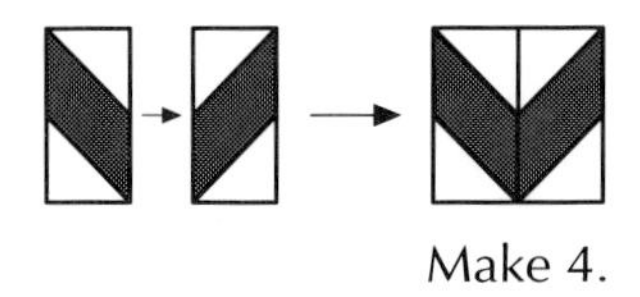

Make 4.

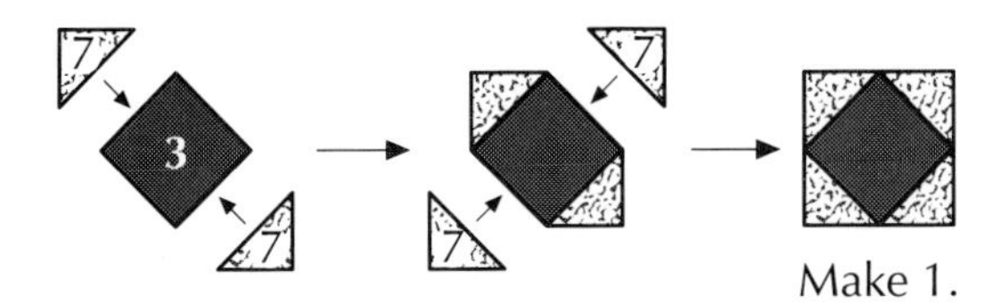

Make 1.

Block Assembly

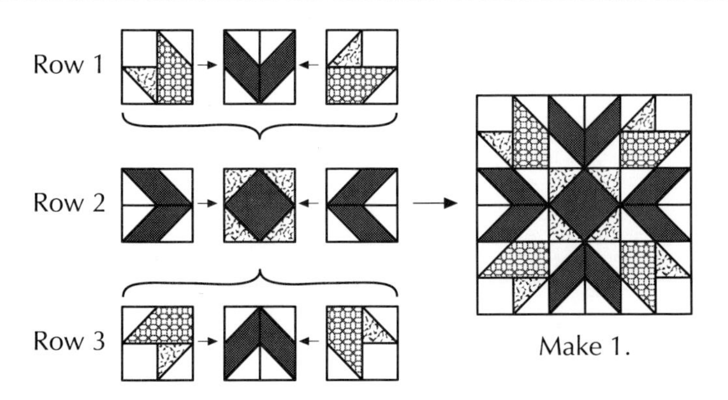

Make 1.

Pine Tree Variation (Block M)

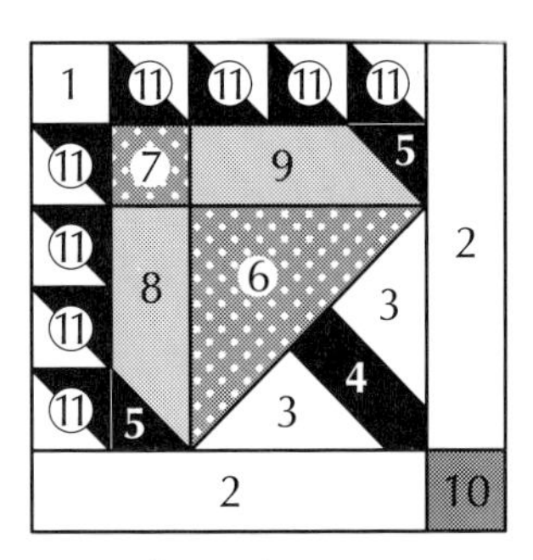

Fabric Placement
Pine Tree Variation
Block M
Finished size: 9"
Note: Piece #11 is a bias square.

Fabric Key

- White
- Dark green
- Medium green
- Light green
- Medium blue

Template Key

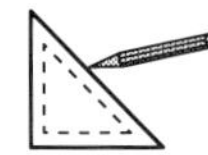

Trace around template.

Templates E, F and F reversed
Templates begin on page 46.

Cutting

Note: The cutting and sewing directions are for four blocks.

From the white fabric, cut:
#1—4 squares, each 2" x 2"
#2—8 rectangles, each 2" x 8"
#3—2 squares, each 5" x 5"; cut twice diagonally for 8 quarter-square triangles
1 square, 12" x 12"*

From the dark green fabric, cut:
#4—4 Template E
#5—4 squares, each $2^{3}/_{8}$" x $2^{3}/_{8}$"; cut once diagonally for 8 half-square triangles
1 square, 12" x 12"*

From the medium green fabric, cut:
#6—2 squares, each $5^{3}/_{8}$" x $5^{3}/_{8}$"; cut once diagonally for 4 half-square triangles
#7—4 squares, each 2" x 2"

From the light green fabric, cut:
#8—4 Template F
#9—4 Template F reversed

From the medium blue fabric, cut:
#10—4 squares, each 2" x 2"

*#11—To make 32 bias-square units, use the 12" squares of white and dark green fabric and the following bias-piecing method.

1. Place the squares right sides together and cut diagonally through the center. Then, cut three 2"-wide bias strips from the resulting triangles. Discard the small remaining triangles or save for another project.

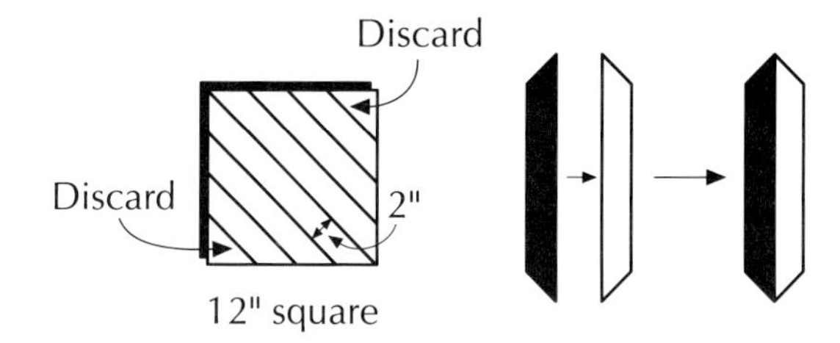

2. Sew the bias strips together in sets, along the long sides.
3. Press the seams toward the dark green strips. Sew the sets together as shown.
4. Cut the 2" x 2" bias squares from the strip-pieced unit, following the cutting sequence in the illustration at the left and using the Bias Square. (See "Making Bias Squares" on pages 7–8.)

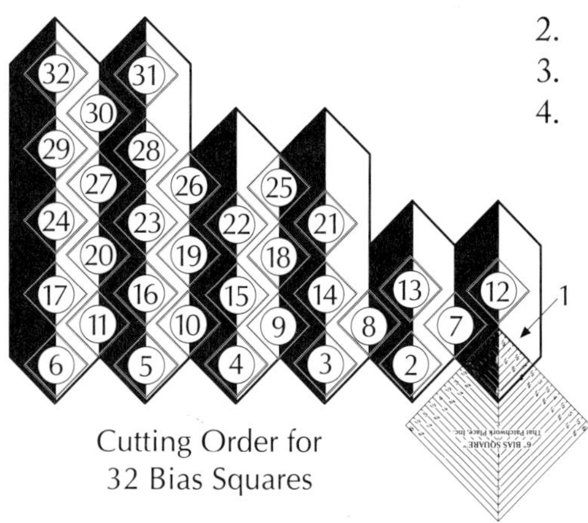

Cutting Order for
32 Bias Squares

Assembly

Piecing Sequence

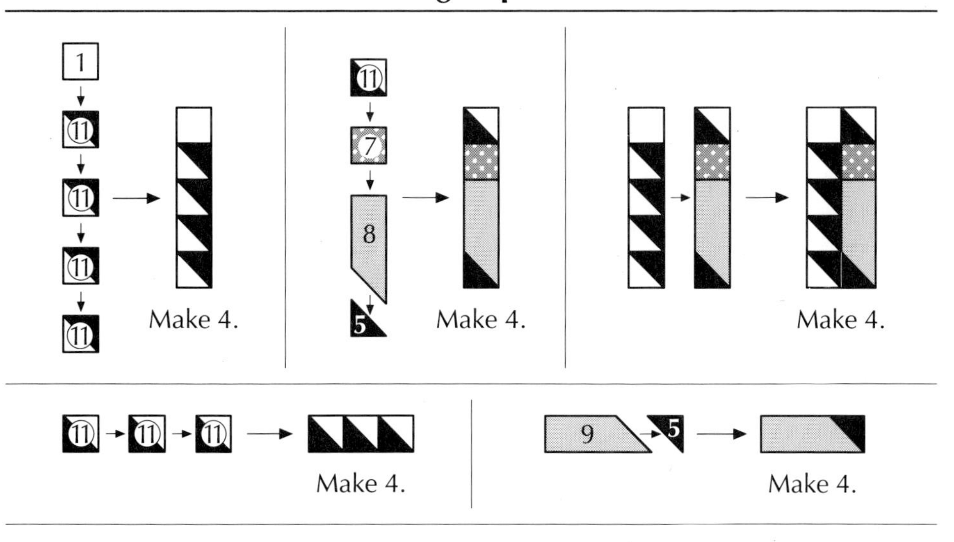

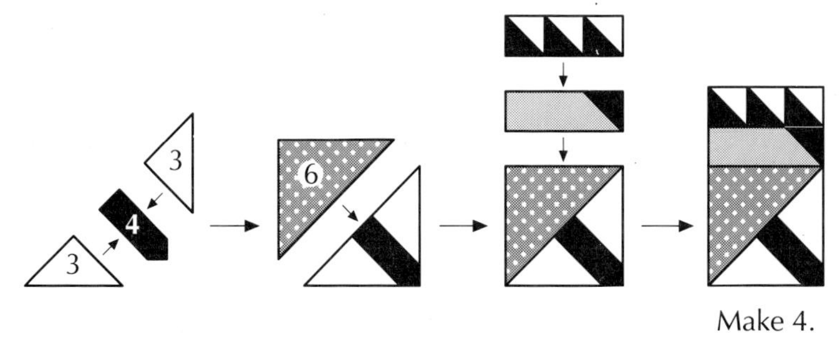

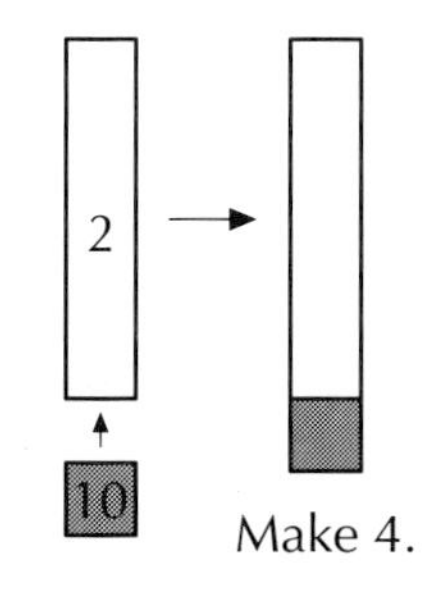

Block Assembly

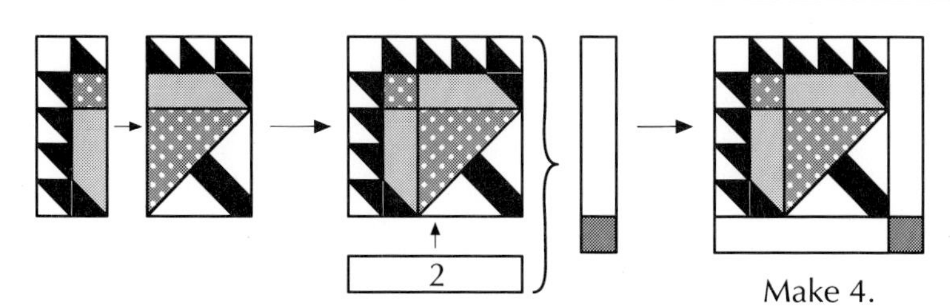

Flying X (Block N)

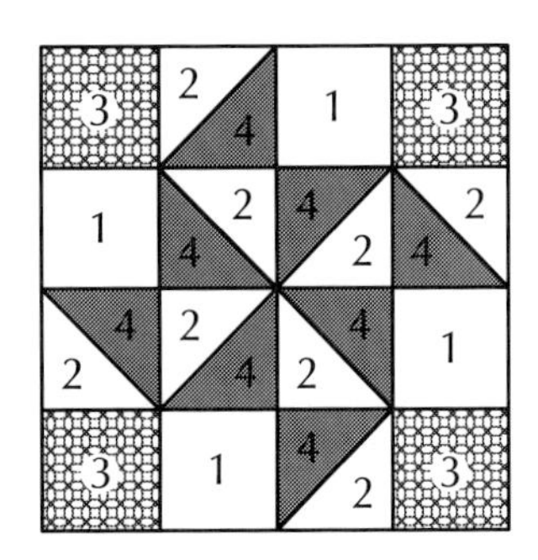

Fabric Placement
Flying X
Block N
Finished size: 9"

Fabric Key

- White
- Dark pink
- Medium blue

Cutting

From the white fabric, cut:
#1—4 squares, each $2\frac{3}{4}$" x $2\frac{3}{4}$"
#2—4 squares, each $3\frac{1}{8}$" x $3\frac{1}{8}$"; cut once diagonally for 8 half-square triangles

From the dark pink fabric, cut:
#3—4 squares, each $2\frac{3}{4}$" x $2\frac{3}{4}$"

From the medium blue fabric, cut:
#4—4 squares, each $3\frac{1}{8}$" x $3\frac{1}{8}$"; cut once diagonally for 8 half-square triangles

Assembly

Piecing Sequence

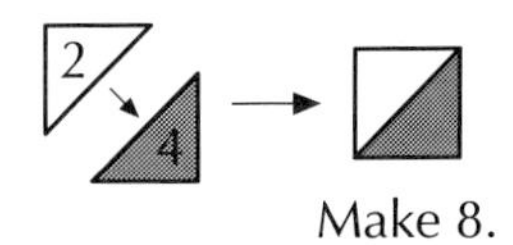

Make 8.

Row Assembly

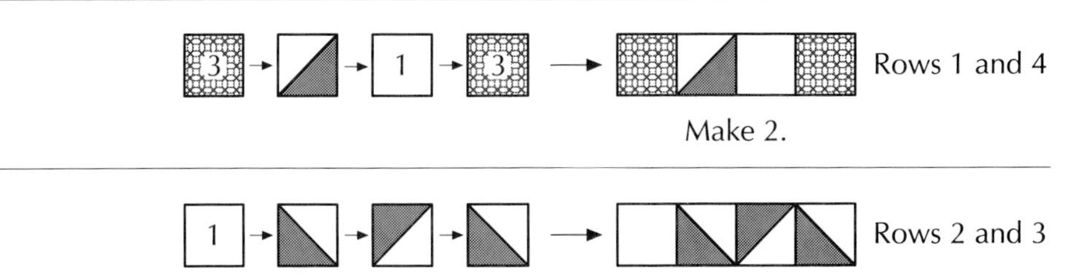

Block Assembly

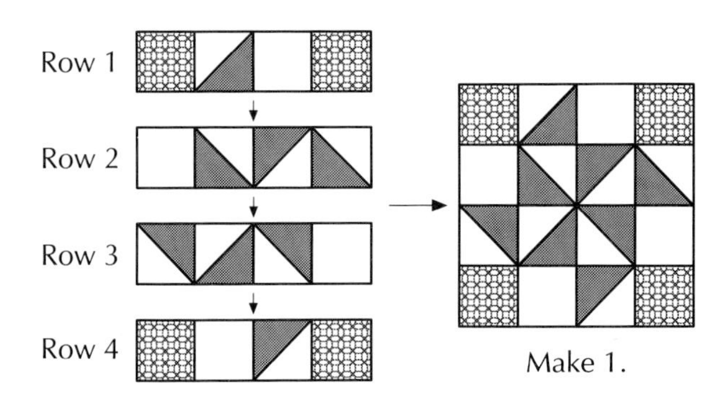

Make 1.

Cutting

From the dark blue fabric, cut:
#1—2 squares, each $5\frac{3}{4}$" x $5\frac{3}{4}$"; cut twice diagonally for 8 quarter-square triangles
#2—2 squares, each $5\frac{3}{8}$" x $5\frac{3}{8}$"; cut once diagonally for 4 half-square triangles

From the medium blue fabric, cut:
#3—2 squares, each $5\frac{3}{4}$" x $5\frac{3}{4}$"; cut twice diagonally for 8 quarter-square triangles
#4—1 square, $6\frac{7}{8}$" x $6\frac{7}{8}$"

From the light blue fabric, cut:
#5—4 squares, each 5" x 5"
#6—2 squares, each $5\frac{3}{4}$" x $5\frac{3}{4}$"; cut twice diagonally for 8 quarter-square triangles

From the light green fabric, cut:
#7—4 Template U

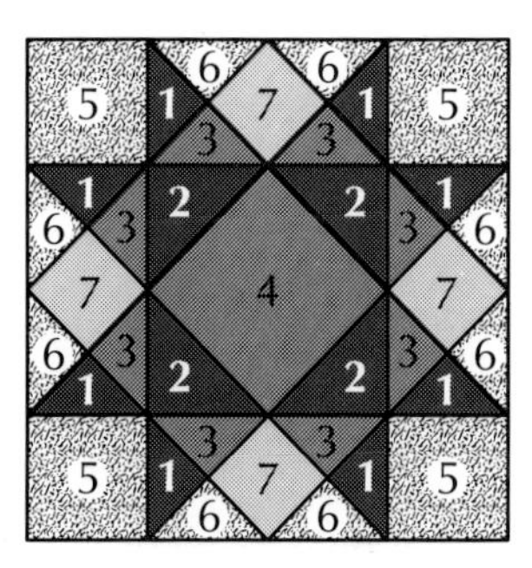

Fabric Placement
Square and Star Variation
Block O
Finished size: 18"

Fabric Key

- Dark blue
- Medium blue
- Light blue
- Light green

Template Key

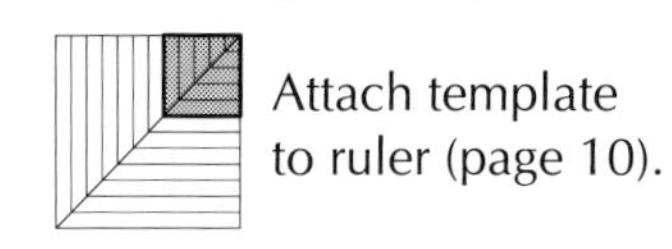

Template U
Templates begin on page 46.

Assembly

Piecing Sequence

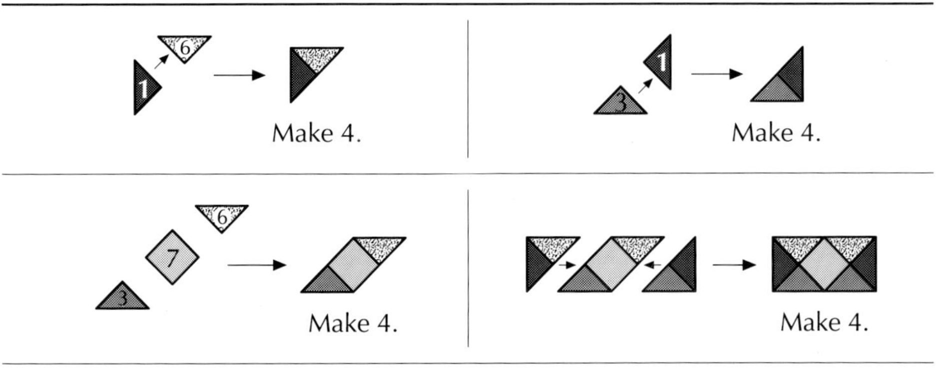

Make 4. Make 4.

Make 4. Make 4.

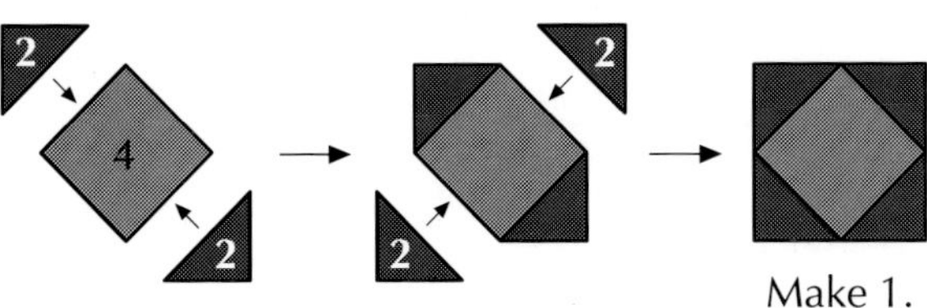

Make 1.

Block Assembly

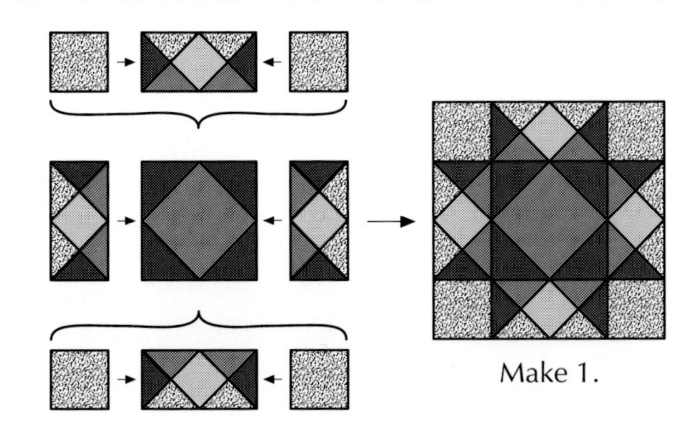

Make 1.

Spool (Block P)

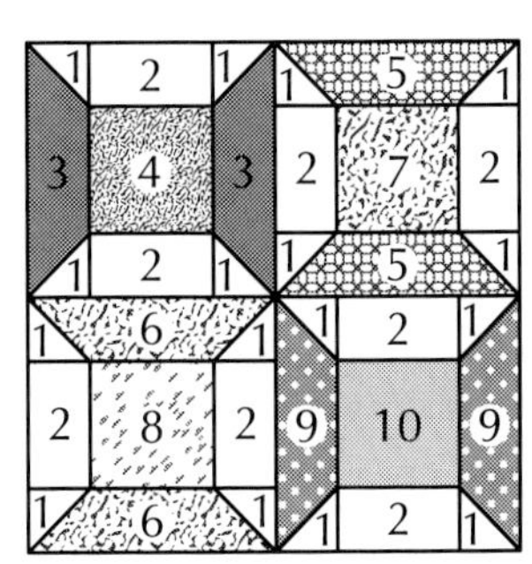

Fabric Placement
Spool
Block P
Finished size: 9"

Fabric Key

- White
- Medium blue
- Light blue
- Dark pink
- Medium pink
- Light pink
- Medium green
- Light green

Template Key

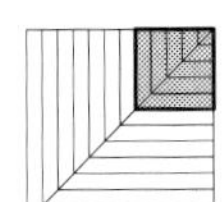

Attach template to ruler (page 10).

Template G
Templates begin on page 46.

Cutting

From the white fabric, cut:
#1—8 squares, each 2" x 2"; cut once diagonally for 16 half-square triangles
#2—8 rectangles, each 1⅝" x 2¾"

From the medium blue fabric, cut:
#3—2 Template G

From the light blue fabric, cut:
#4—1 square, 2¾" x 2¾"

From the dark pink fabric, cut:
#5—2 Template G

From the medium pink fabric, cut:
#6—2 Template G
#7—1 square, 2¾" x 2¾"

From the light pink fabric, cut:
#8—1 square, 2¾" x 2¾"

From the medium green fabric, cut:
#9—2 Template G

From the light green fabric, cut:
#10—1 square, 2¾" x 2¾"

Assembly

Piecing Sequence

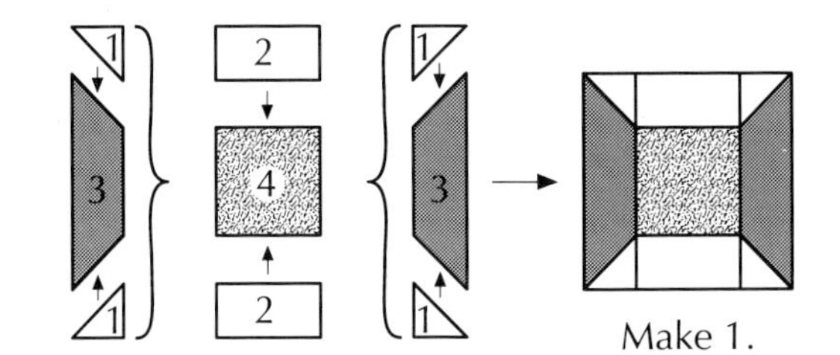

Make 1.

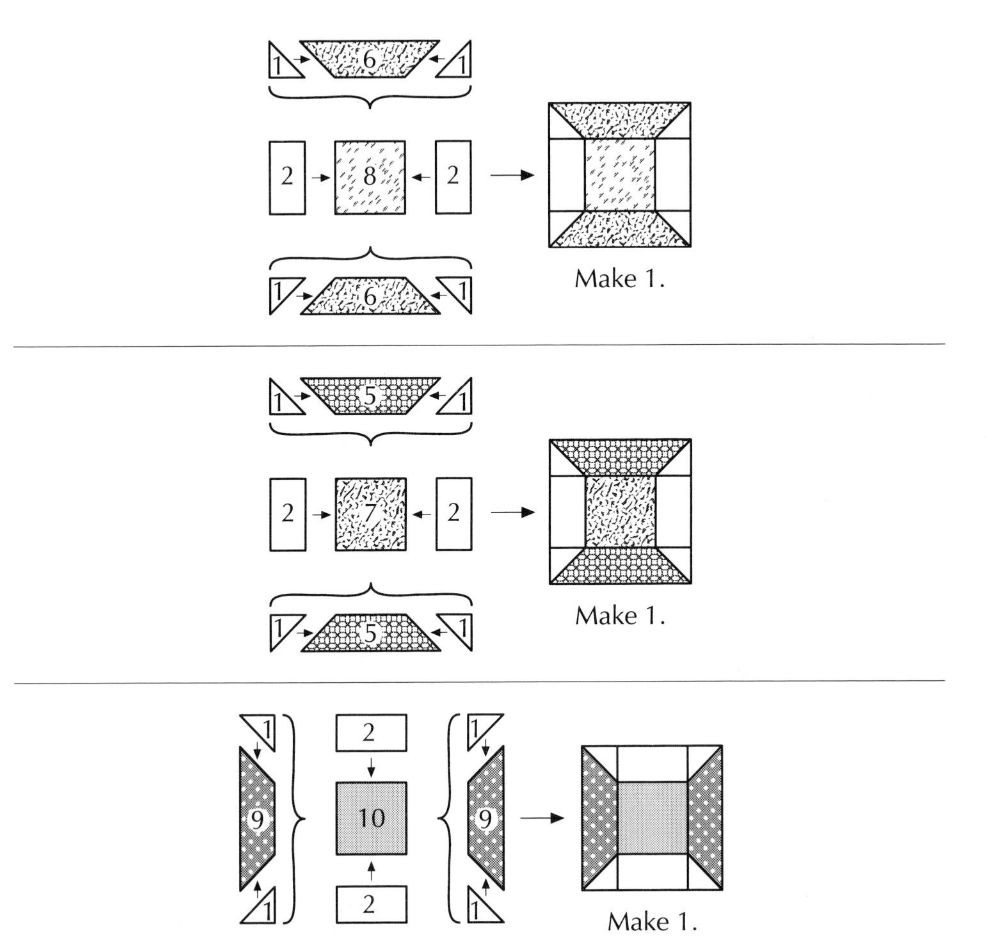

Block Assembly

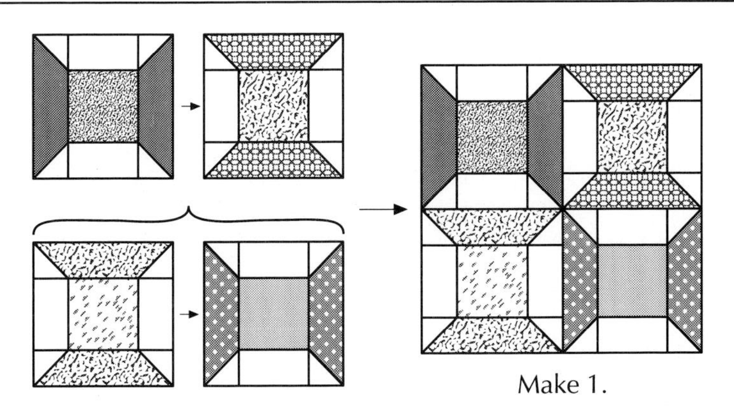

Make 1.

Grape Basket (Block Q)

Fabric Placement
Grape Basket
Block Q
Finished size: 9"
Note: Pieces #9 and #10 are bias squares.

Fabric Key

- White
- Dark pink
- Medium pink
- Light pink

Template Key

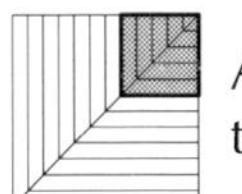

Attach template to ruler (page 10).

Templates K, L, M, N
Templates begin on page 46.

Cutting

Note: The cutting and sewing directions are for two blocks.

From the white fabric, cut:
#1—2 Template K
#2—4 Template L
#3—4 Template N
#4—4 rectangles, each $5\frac{7}{8}$" x $2\frac{5}{16}$"*
*See "Traditional Templates" on page 8.

From the dark pink fabric, cut:
#5—4 Template M

From the medium pink fabric, cut:
#6—2 Template L
#7—4 Template M

From the light pink fabric, cut:
#8—4 Template M

#9—To make bias squares, cut 1 bias strip, $2\frac{1}{4}$" x 11", from each of the white and dark pink fabrics. Sew the strips together on the long side. Press the seam toward the dark pink strip. Center Template K as illustrated and cut 2 squares. Remove the center seam of the leftover piece; turn the pieces around. Stitch a new seam and cut 2 more squares.

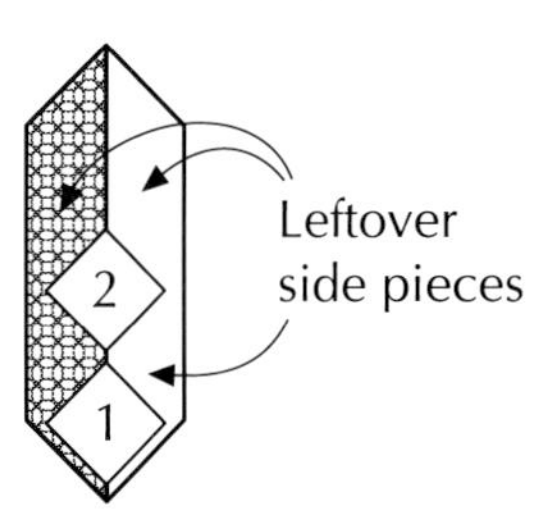

Stitch strips together. Center Template K as illustrated and cut 2 squares.

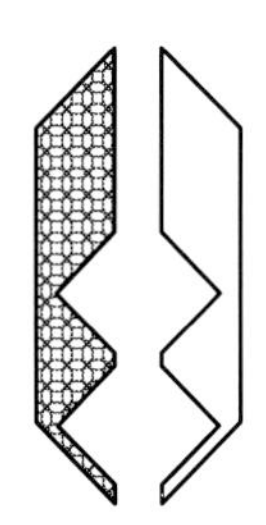

Remove seam from leftover pieces.

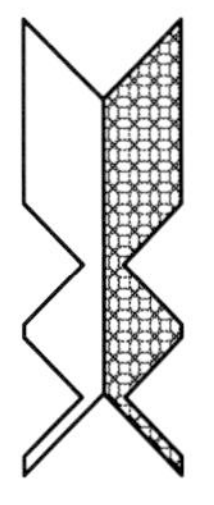

Turn pieces around; stitch new seam.

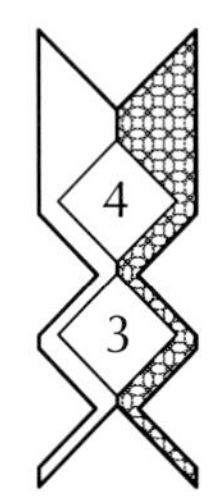

Cut pieces 3 and 4.

#10—To make bias squares, cut 1 bias strip, $2\frac{1}{4}$" x 21", from each of the white and light pink fabrics. Join on the long side. Center Template K as shown above and cut 5 squares. Seam the leftover side pieces and cut 5 more squares for a total of 10.

Assembly

Piecing Sequence

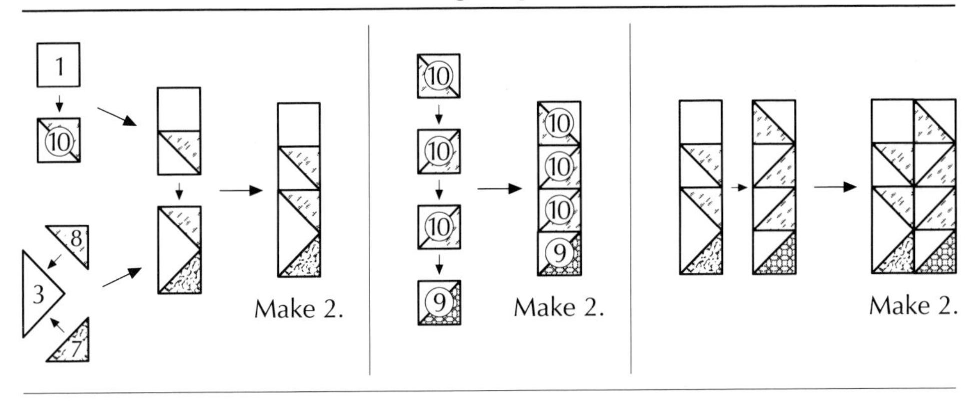

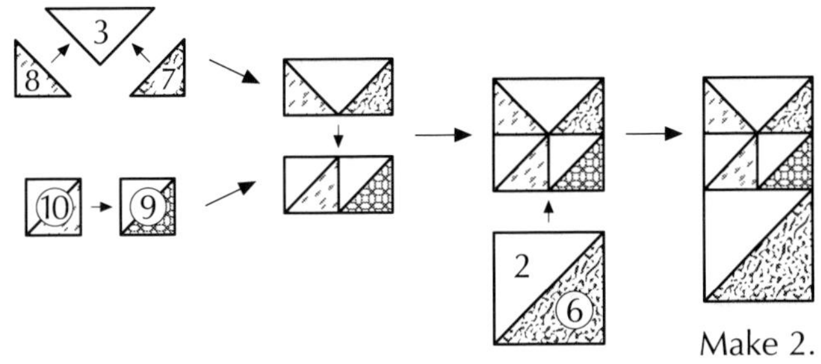

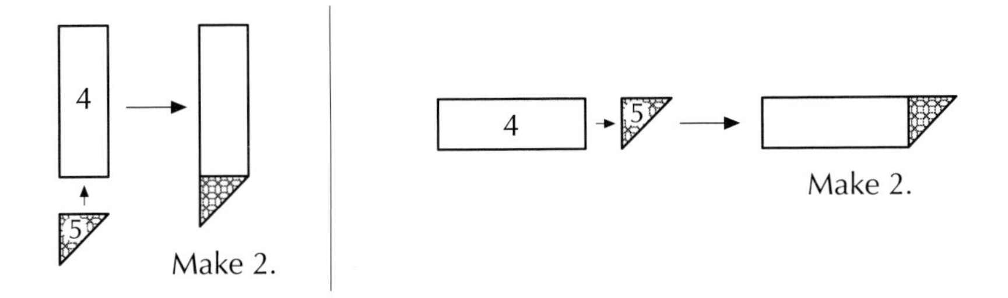

Block Assembly

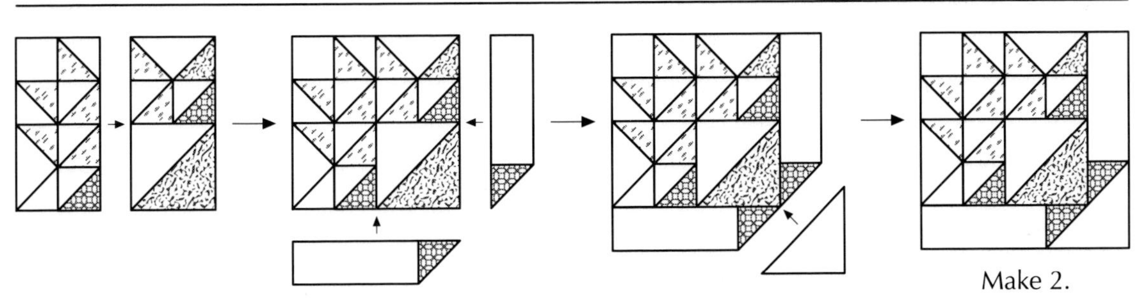

Bouquet Variation I (Block R)

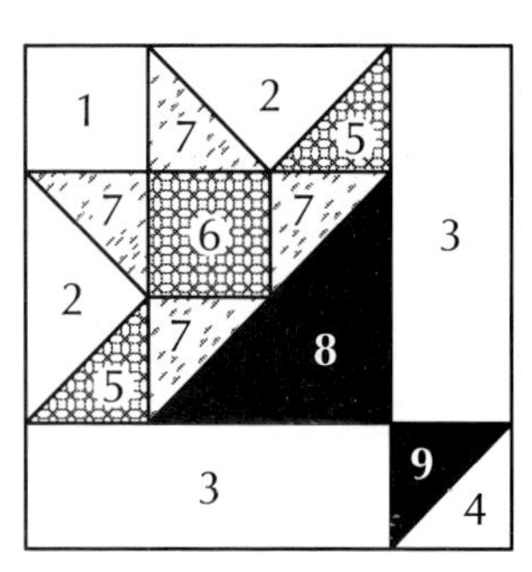

Fabric Placement
Bouquet Variation I
Block R
Finished size: 9"

Fabric Key

- White
- Dark pink
- Light pink
- Dark green

Cutting

Note: The cutting and sewing directions are for two blocks.

From the white fabric, cut:
#1—2 squares, each $2^3/_4$" x $2^3/_4$"
#2—1 square, $5^3/_4$" x $5^3/_4$"; cut twice diagonally for 4 quarter-square triangles
#3—4 rectangles, each $7^1/_4$" x $2^3/_4$"
#4—1 square, $3^1/_8$" x $3^1/_8$"; cut once diagonally for 2 half-square triangles

From the dark pink fabric, cut:
#5—2 squares, each $3^1/_8$" x $3^1/_8$"; cut once diagonally for 4 half-square triangles
#6—2 squares, each $2^3/_4$" x $2^3/_4$"

From the light pink fabric, cut:
#7—4 squares, each $3^1/_8$" x $3^1/_8$"; cut once diagonally for 8 half-square triangles

From the dark green fabric, cut:
#8—1 square, $5^3/_8$" x $5^3/_8$"; cut once diagonally for 2 half-square triangles
#9—1 square, $3^1/_8$" x $3^1/_8$"; cut once diagonally for 2 half-square triangles

Assembly

Piecing Sequence

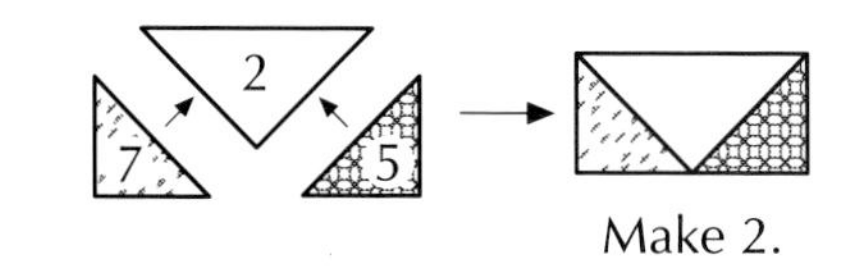

Make 2.

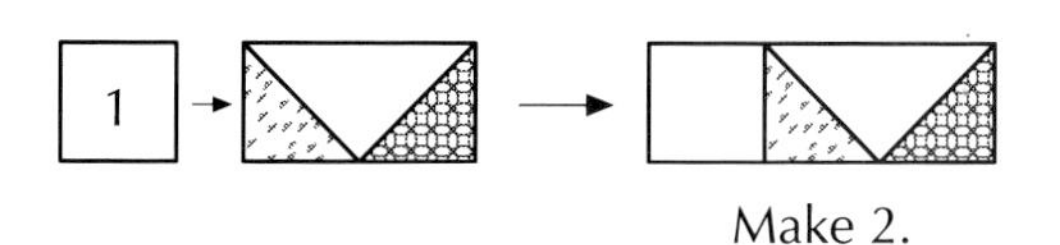

Make 2.

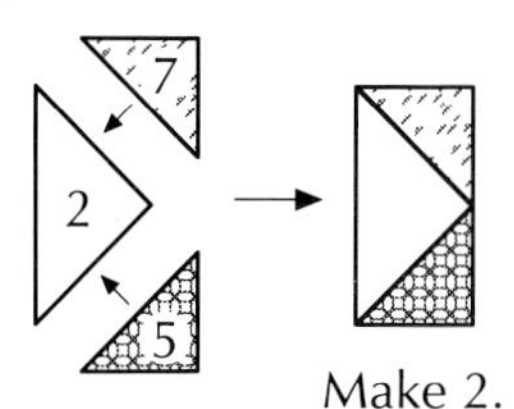

Make 2.

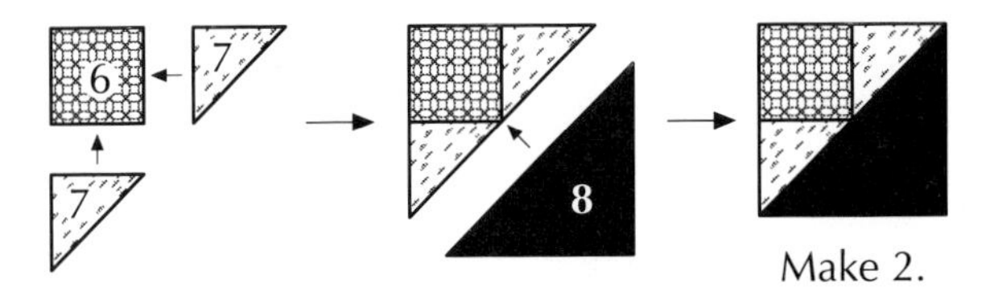

Make 2.

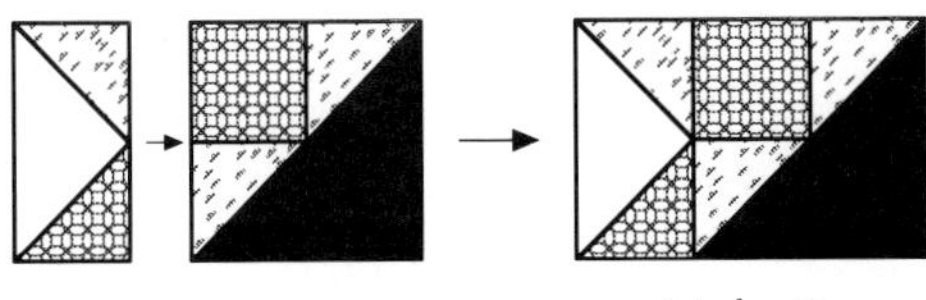

Make 2.

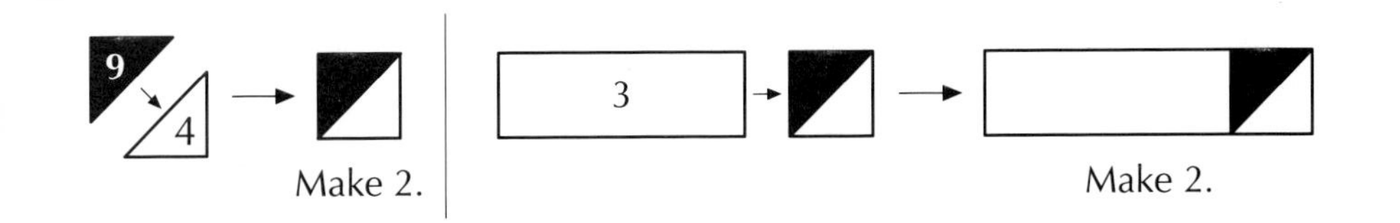

Make 2.

Make 2.

Block Assembly

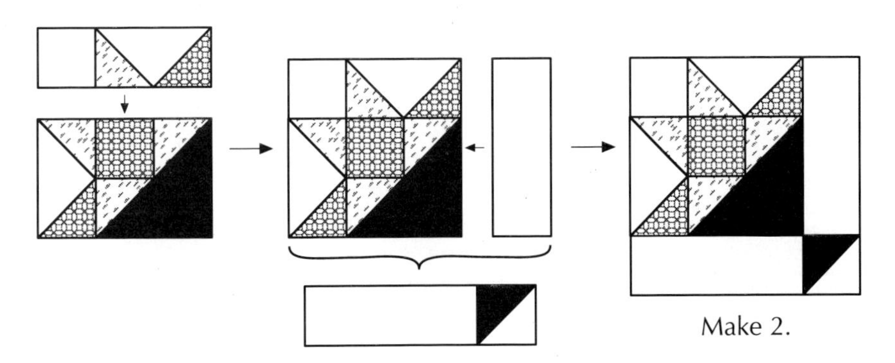

Make 2.

Bouquet Variation II (Block S)

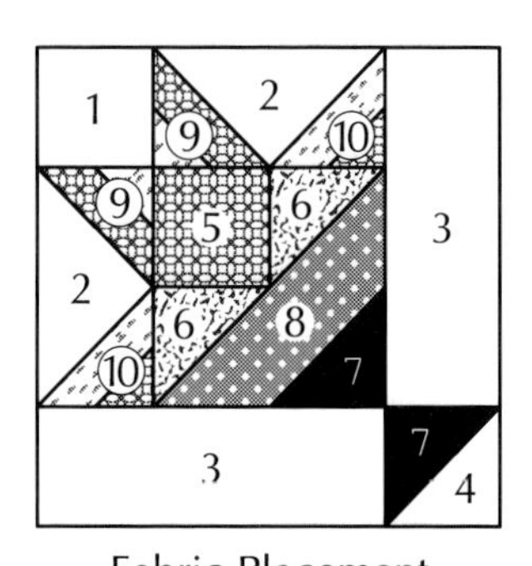

Fabric Placement
Bouquet Variation II
Block S
Finished size: 9"
Note: Pieces #9 and #10 are made from seamed fabric strips. See instructions below right and refer to illustration.

Fabric Key

- White
- Dark pink
- Medium pink
- Dark green
- Medium green
- Light pink

Template Key

Trace around template.

Template I

Attach template to ruler (page 10).

Template J
Templates begin on page 46.

Cutting

Note: The cutting and sewing directions are for two blocks.

From the white fabric, cut:
#1—2 squares, each $2\frac{3}{4}$" x $2\frac{3}{4}$"
#2—1 square, $5\frac{3}{4}$" x $5\frac{3}{4}$"; cut twice diagonally for 4 quarter-square triangles
#3—4 rectangles, each $7\frac{1}{4}$" x $2\frac{3}{4}$"
#4—1 square, $3\frac{1}{8}$" x $3\frac{1}{8}$"; cut once diagonally for 2 half-square triangles

From the dark pink fabric, cut:
#5—2 squares, each $2\frac{3}{4}$" x $2\frac{3}{4}$"

From the medium pink fabric, cut:
#6—2 squares, each $3\frac{1}{8}$" x $3\frac{1}{8}$"; cut once diagonally for 4 half-square triangles

From the dark green fabric, cut:
#7—2 squares, $3\frac{1}{8}$" x $3\frac{1}{8}$"; cut once diagonally for 4 half-square triangles

From the medium green fabric, cut:
#8—2 Template J

Make seamed fabric strips* and cut:
9—4 Template I (dark pink at the base of the triangle)
#10—4 Template I (light pink at the base of the triangle)

***To make seamed fabric strips for Template I:**

1. Cut 2 bias strips, each $1\frac{3}{8}$" wide and at least 13" long, from the dark pink and light pink fabrics.
2. Sew a dark pink strip to a light pink strip on the long side. Make 2 sets. Press the seams toward the dark pink strips.
3. On both sets, center Template I on the indicated seam line and mark and cut as shown.

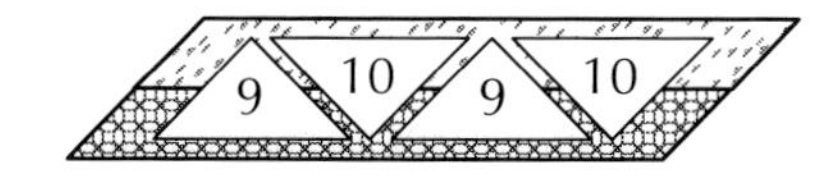

Assembly

Piecing Sequence

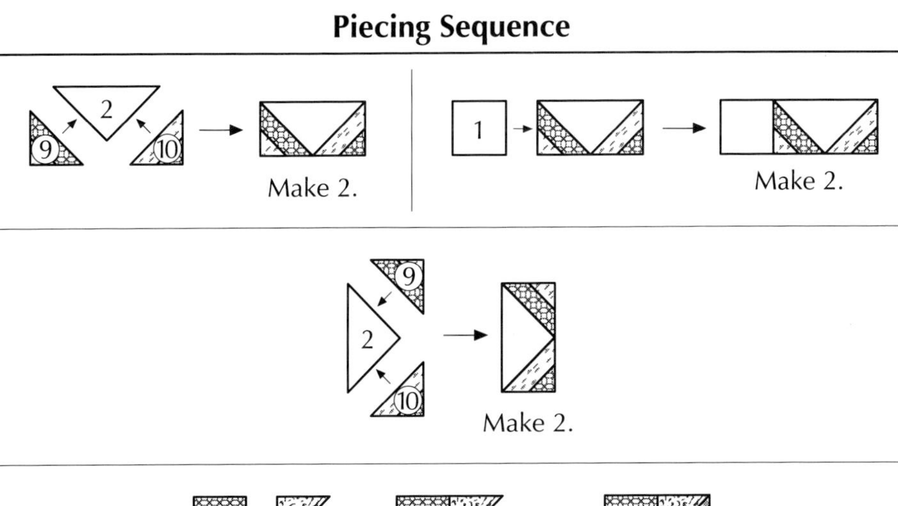

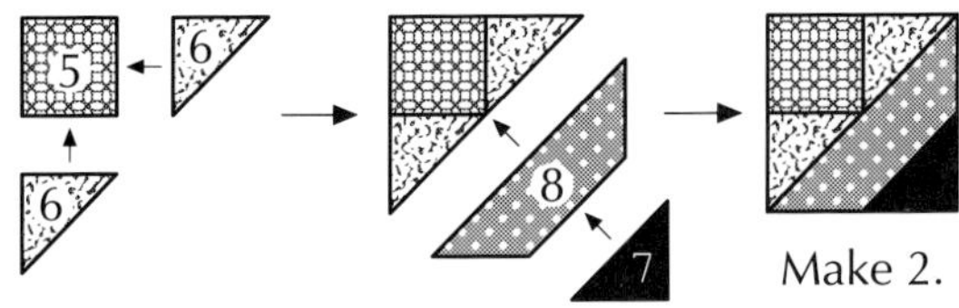

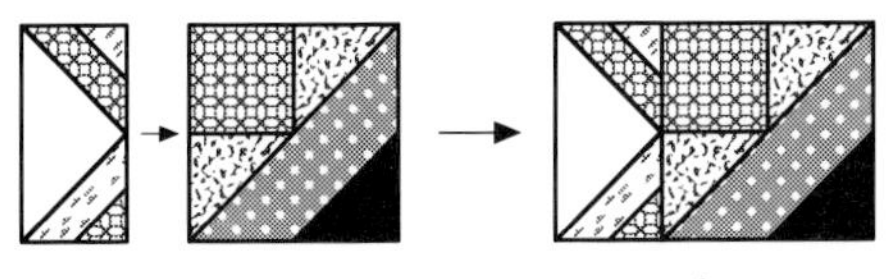

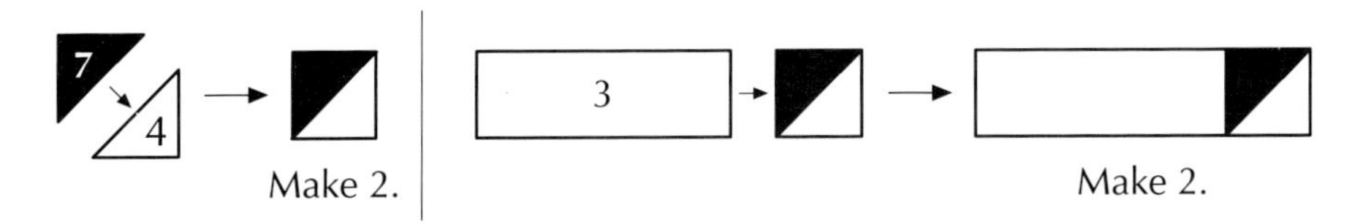

Block Assembly

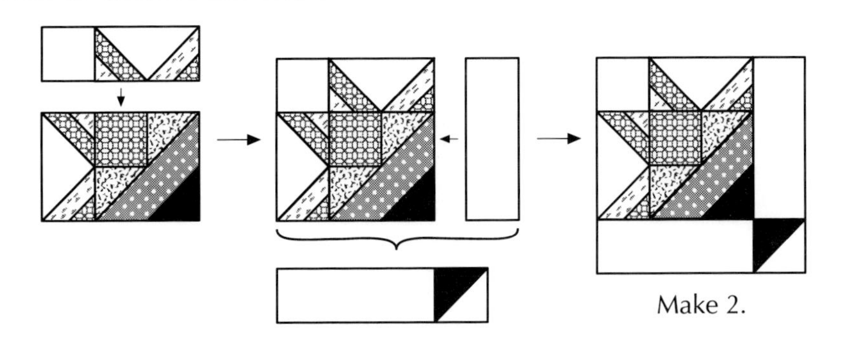

Flower Basket Variation (Block T)

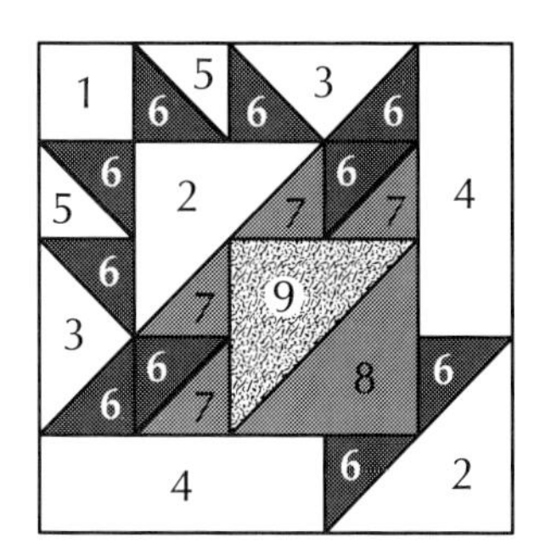

Fabric Placement
Flower Basket Variation
Block T
Finished size: 9"

Fabric Key

- White
- Dark blue
- Medium blue
- Light blue

Template Key

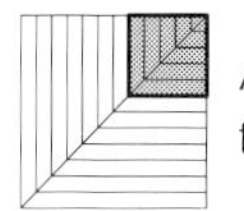

Attach template to ruler (page 10).

Templates K, L, M, N
Templates begin on page 46.

Cutting

Note: The cutting and sewing directions are for two blocks.

From the white fabric, cut:
#1—2 Template K
#2—4 Template L
#3—4 Template N
#4—4 rectangles, each $5\frac{7}{8}$" x $2\frac{5}{16}$"*
#5—4 Template M
*See "Traditional Templates" on page 8.

From the dark blue fabric, cut:
#6—20 Template M

From the medium blue fabric, cut:
#7—8 Template M
#8—2 Template L

From the light blue fabric, cut:
#9—2 Template L

Assembly

Piecing Sequence

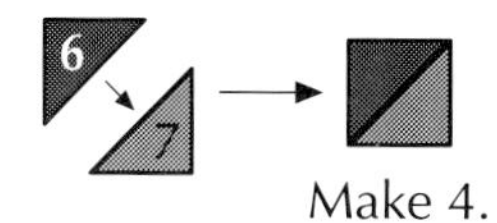

Make 4.

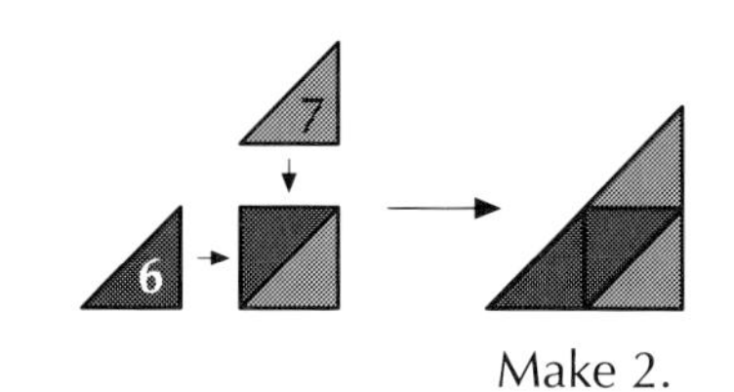

Make 2.

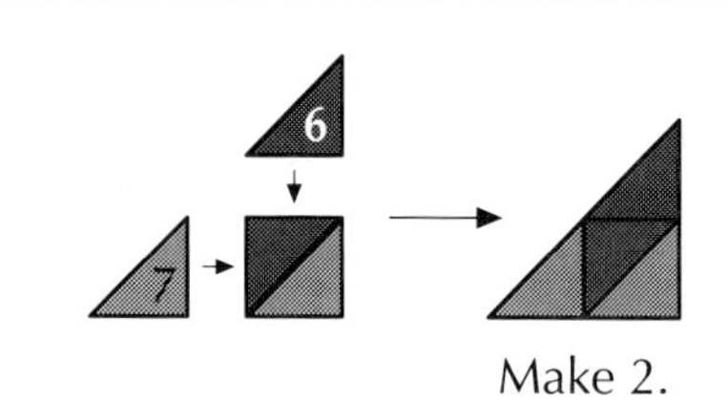

Make 2.

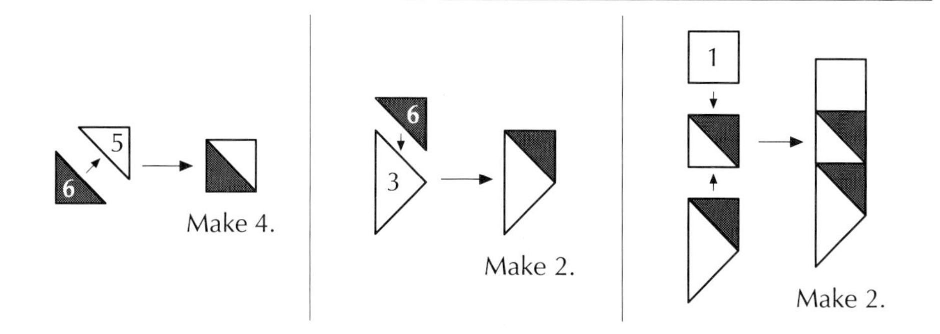

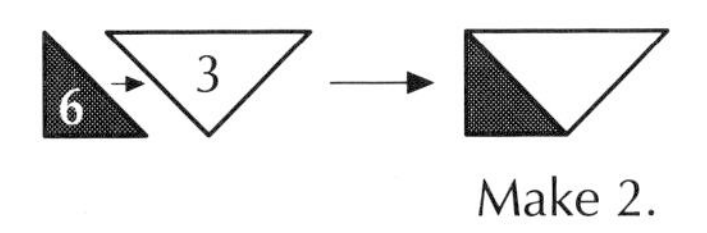

Make 2.

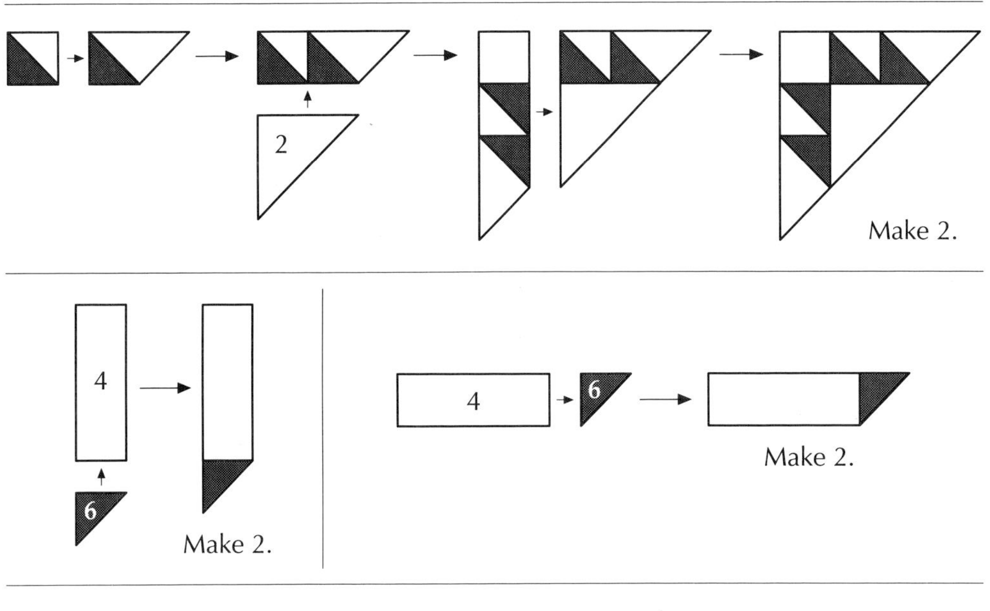

Make 2.

Make 2.

Make 2.

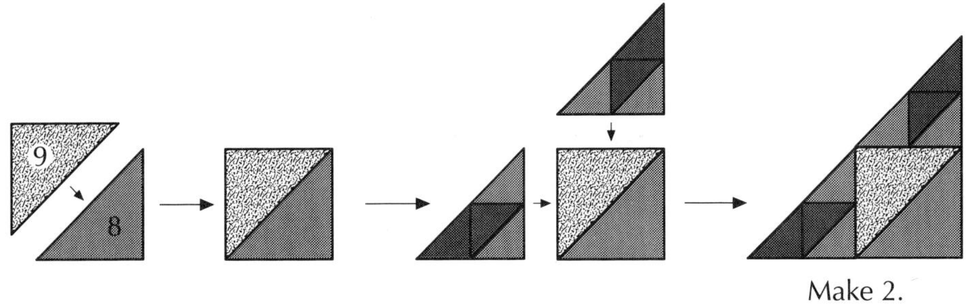

Make 2.

Block Assembly

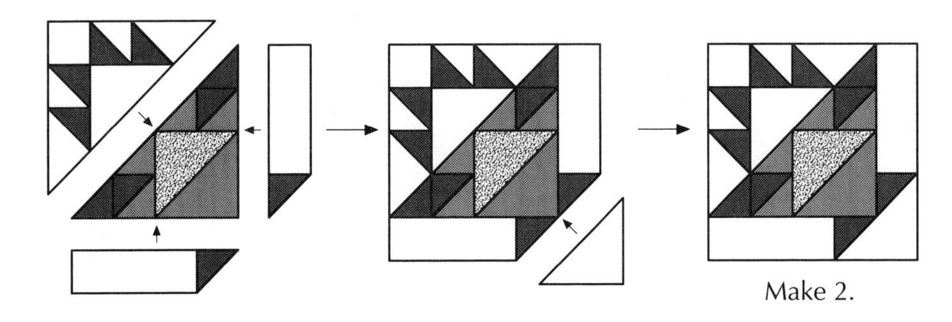
Make 2.

Goose Tracks Variation (Block U)

Fabric Placement
Goose Tracks Variation
Block U
Finished size: 9"

Fabric Key

- White
- Dark pink
- Medium pink
- Light pink
- Dark green
- Medium green

Template Key

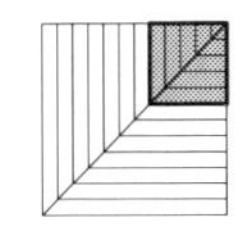

Attach template to ruler (page 10).

Templates K, M, O, Q, Q reversed
Templates begin on page 46.

Cutting

From the white fabric, cut:
#1—4 rectangles, each $2\frac{5}{16}$" x $4\frac{1}{16}$"*
#2—4 Template K
#3—8 Template O
*See "Traditional Templates" on page 8.

From the dark pink fabric, cut:
#4—8 Template O

From the medium pink fabric, cut:
#5—4 Template Q
#6—4 Template Q reversed

From the light pink fabric, cut:
#7—4 Template M

From the dark green fabric, cut:
#8—1 Template K

From the medium green fabric, cut:
#9—4 Template M

Assembly

Piecing Sequence

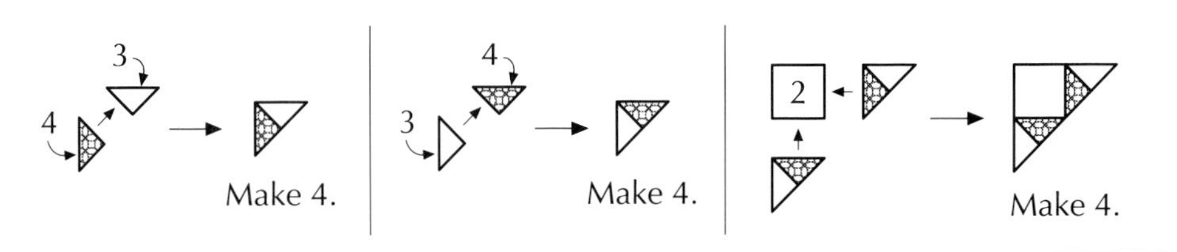

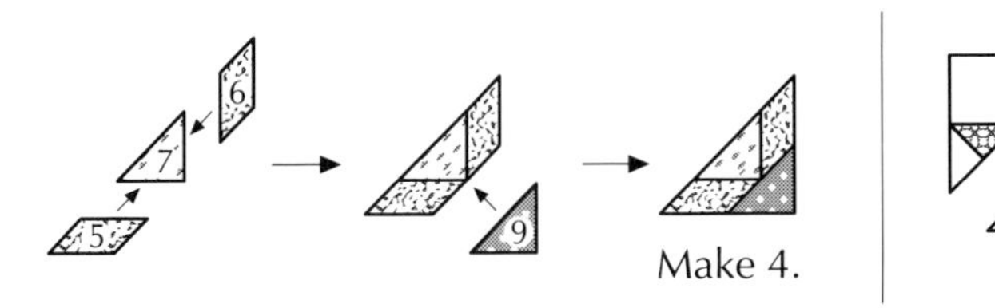

Block Assembly

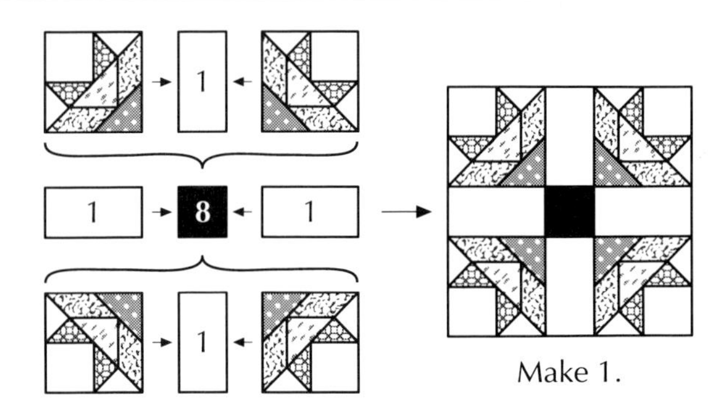

Cutting

From the white fabric, cut:
#1—12 Template M
#2—4 Template K
#3—4 Template O

From the dark pink fabric, cut:
#4—4 Template M
#5—1 Template K
#6—8 Template O

From the dark green fabric, cut:
#7—4 Template P

From the medium green fabric, cut:
#8—4 Template O

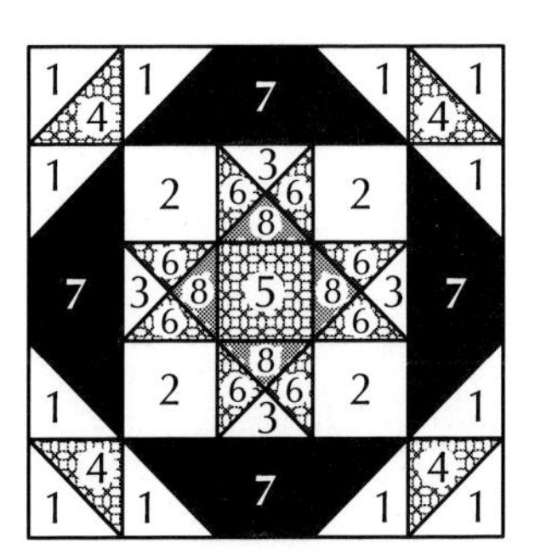

Fabric Placement
Square and a Half
Block V
Finished size: 9"

Fabric Key

- White
- Dark pink
- Dark green
- Medium green

Template Key

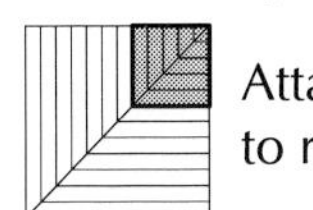

Attach template to ruler (page 10).

Templates K, M, O, P
Templates begin on page 46.

Assembly

Piecing Sequence

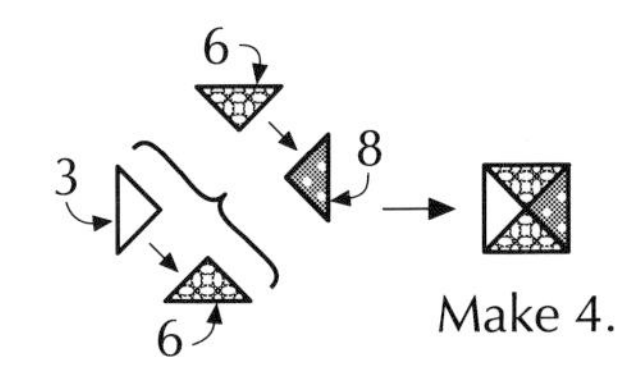

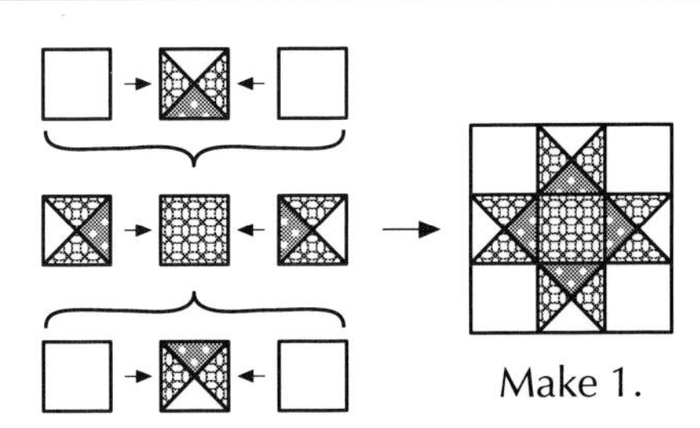

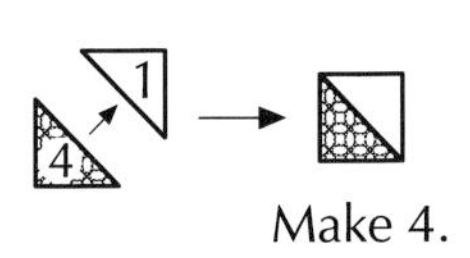

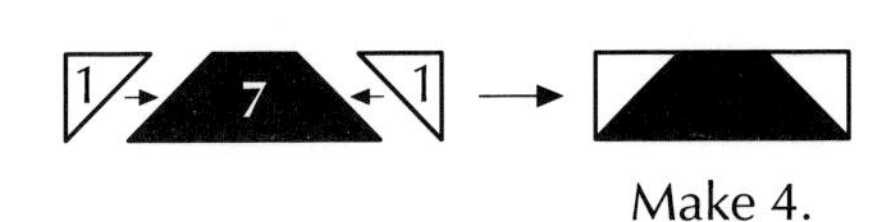

Block Assembly

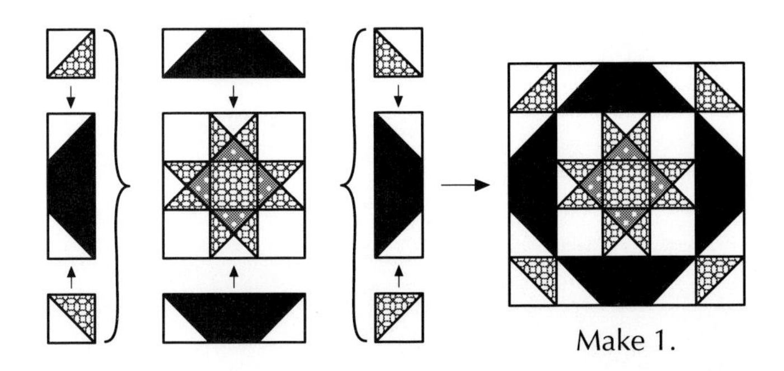

Pieced House (Block W)

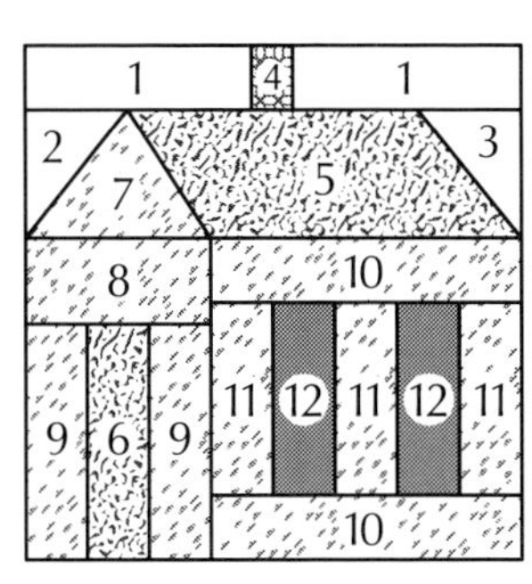

Fabric Placement
Pieced House
Block W
Finished size: 9"

Fabric Key

- White
- Dark pink
- Medium pink
- Light pink
- Medium blue

Template Key

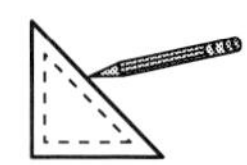

Trace around template.

Templates R, S, S reversed, T
Templates begin on page 46.

Cutting

From the white fabric, cut:
#1—2 rectangles, each 4⅝" x 1⅝"
#2—1 Template S
#3—1 Template S reversed

From the dark pink fabric, cut:
#4—1 rectangle, 1¼" x 1⅝"

From the medium pink fabric, cut:
#5—1 Template R

Caution: *Both sides of the roof do not have the same angle. Be sure to mark the wrong side of the fabric with the wrong side of the template facing up and with the arrow pointing to the top of the block.*

#6—1 rectangle, 4⅝" x 1⅝"

From the light pink fabric, cut:
#7—1 Template T

Caution: *Both sides of the triangle do not have the same angle. Be sure to mark on the wrong side of the fabric with the wrong side of the template facing up and with the arrow pointing to the top of the block.*

#8—1 rectangle, 3⅞" x 2"
Hint: Cut a strip of fabric 1⅝" wide to cut the following rectangles:
#9—2 rectangles, each 4⅝" x 1⅝"
#10—2 rectangles, each 6⅛" x 1⅝"
#11—3 rectangles, each 3⅞" x 1⅝"

From the medium blue fabric, cut:
#12—2 rectangles, each 3⅞" x 1⅝"

Assembly

Piecing Sequence

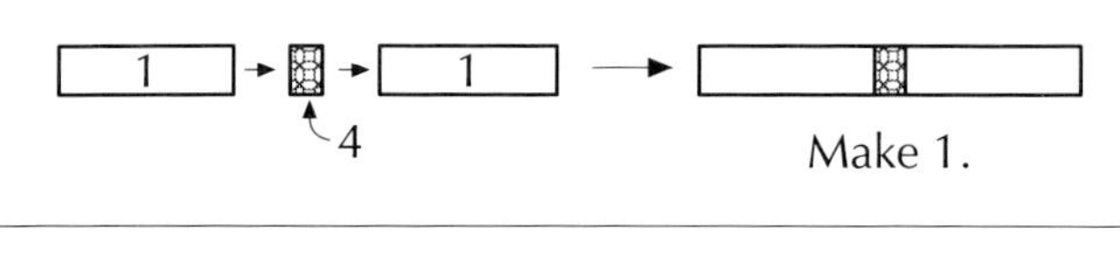

Make 1.

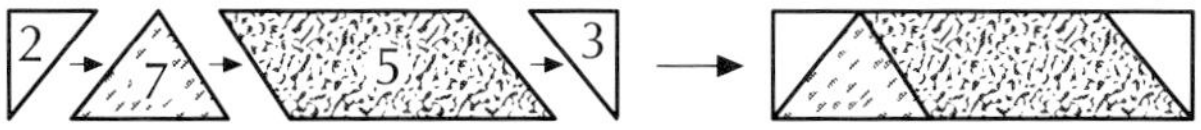

Make 1.

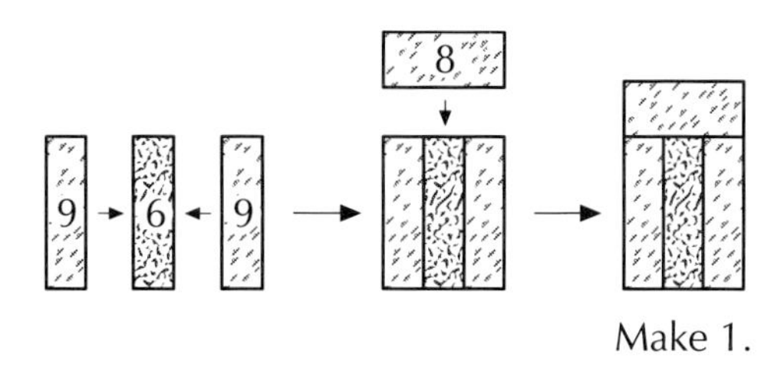

Make 1.

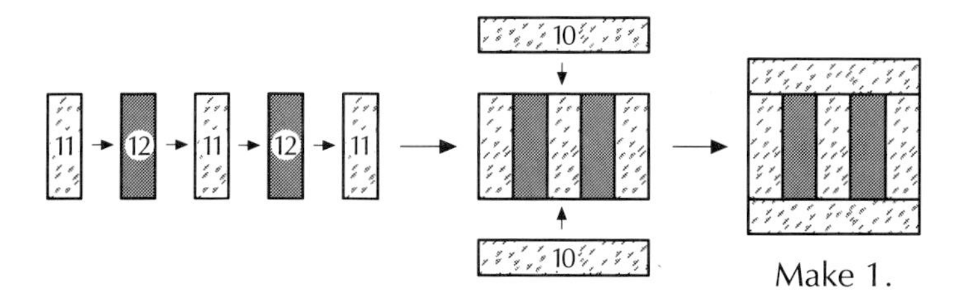

Make 1.

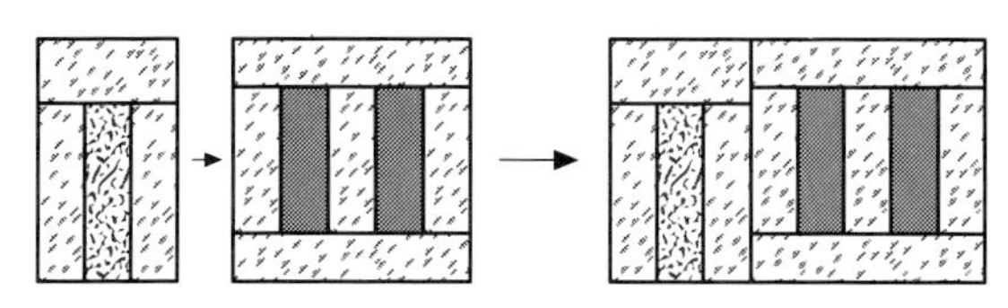

Make 1.

Block Assembly

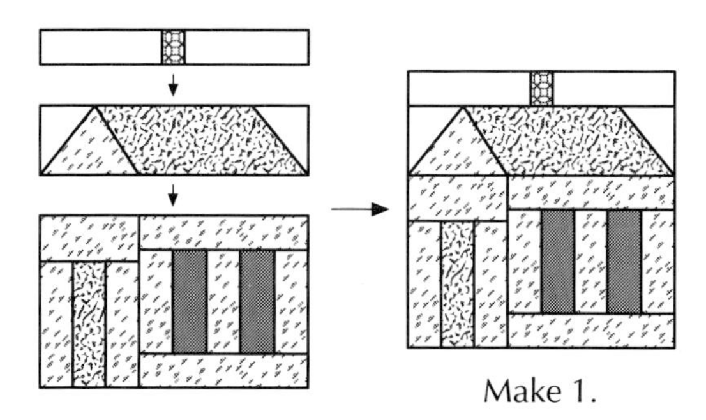

Make 1.

Quilt Top Assembly and Finishing

Joining the Blocks

It is time to join the blocks together to form the center of the quilt. Piece the quilt top blocks in the 9 units shown; then join the units.

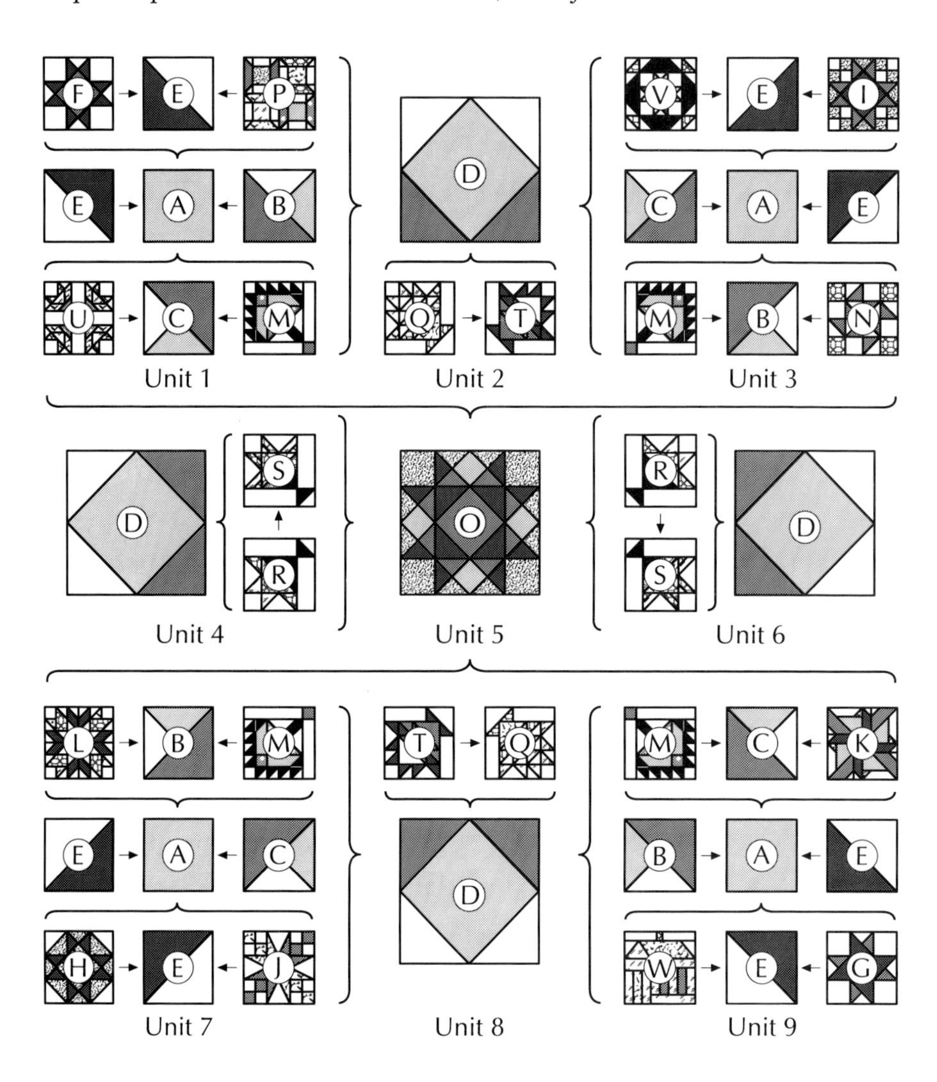

Adding the Borders

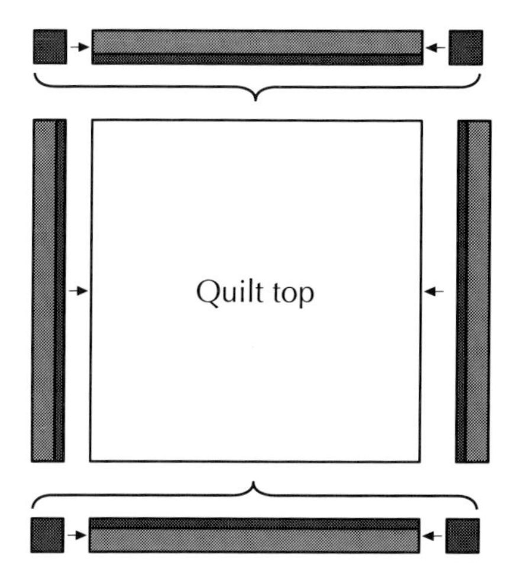

1. Sew each dark blue border strip to a medium blue border strip for 4 sets.
2. Lay the quilt top flat and measure the distance vertically through the center. It should measure about 72½".
3. Cut 2 of the pieced border strips this length. Fold these border strips in half, then in quarters, and mark the folds with pins. Fold the quilt top in half, then in quarters, and mark the midpoint and quarter-point locations on the two sides of the quilt with pins.
4. Matching the pins on the border strips to the pins on the sides of the quilt top, pin the pieced border strips to the quilt top. Stitch.
5. Measure the distance through the center of the quilt top across the width of the quilt from border seam line to border seam line. Cut the remaining 2 pieced border strips this measurement plus ½". Sew a 7½" dark blue square to each end of each strip.
6. Fold the pieced border strips and the quilt top in half, then in quarters, and mark the folds with pins as before.
7. Pin the bottom and top strips to the quilt top, matching the pins. Stitch. Press seams toward the border.

Finishing the Quilt

1. Mark quilting designs now or wait and mark as you quilt if that is your preference.
2. Prepare the backing. First remove the selvages from the 8 yards of prewashed backing fabric. Cut it into 3 equal lengths, each approximately 94" long. Stitch the 3 pieces together as shown.

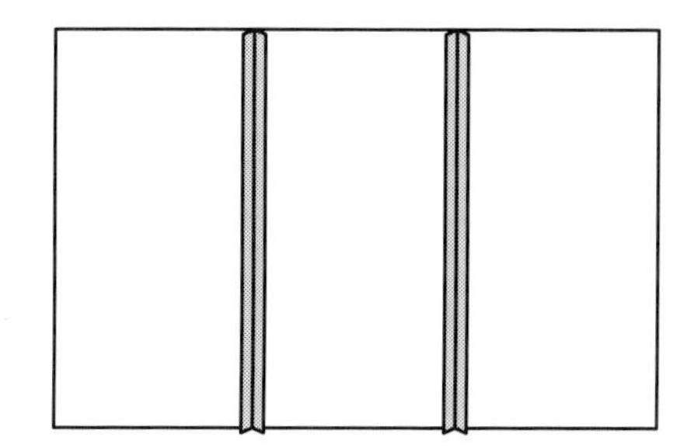

3. Layer the quilt top with the batting and backing; baste. After the basting is completed, trim the backing to 3"–4" all around, then bring the excess backing fabric from the back around to the front and baste it over the exposed batting.
4. Quilt as desired. For information on planning your quilting, see *Loving Stitches* by Jeana Kimball.
5. Bind the edges. See *Happy Endings* by Mimi Dietrich for step-by-step directions.
6. For a finishing touch, attach a label to the back of the quilt with your name and date and any other information you would like to add.

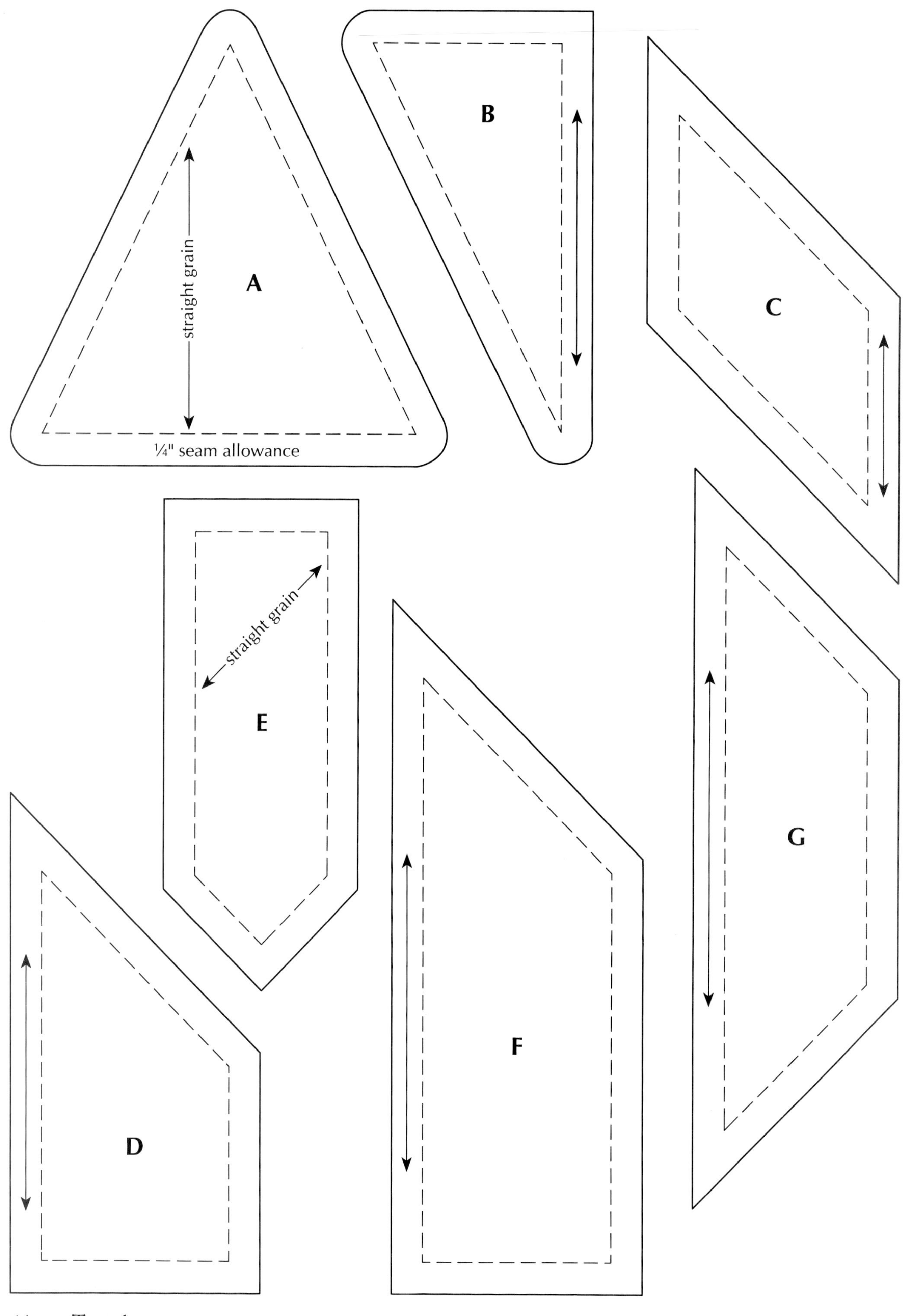
A
straight grain
¼" seam allowance
B
C
E
straight grain
D
F
G

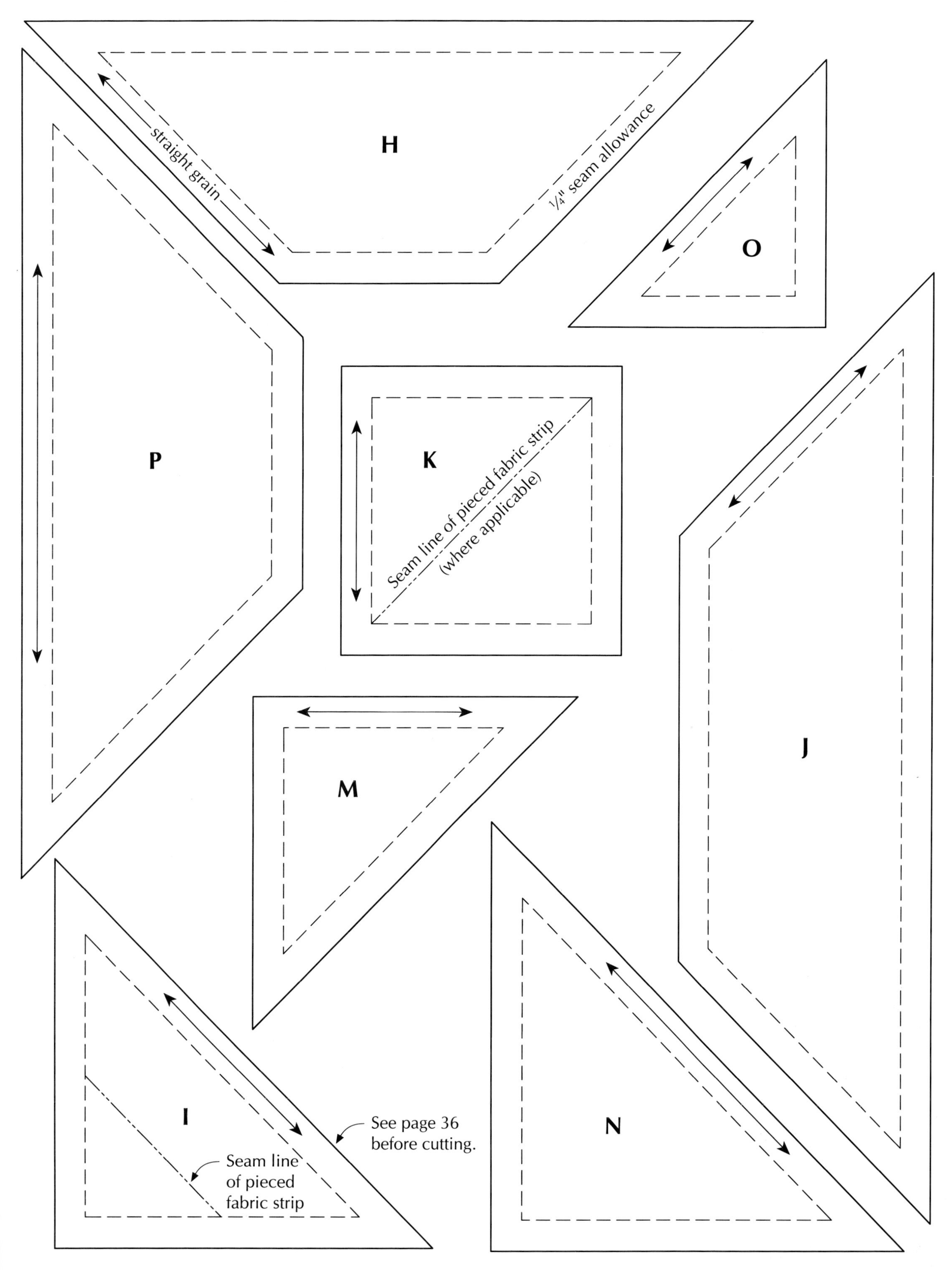
H
straight grain
$\frac{1}{4}$" seam allowance
O
P
K
Seam line of pieced fabric strip
(where applicable)
J
M
I
See page 36
before cutting.
Seam line
of pieced
fabric strip
N

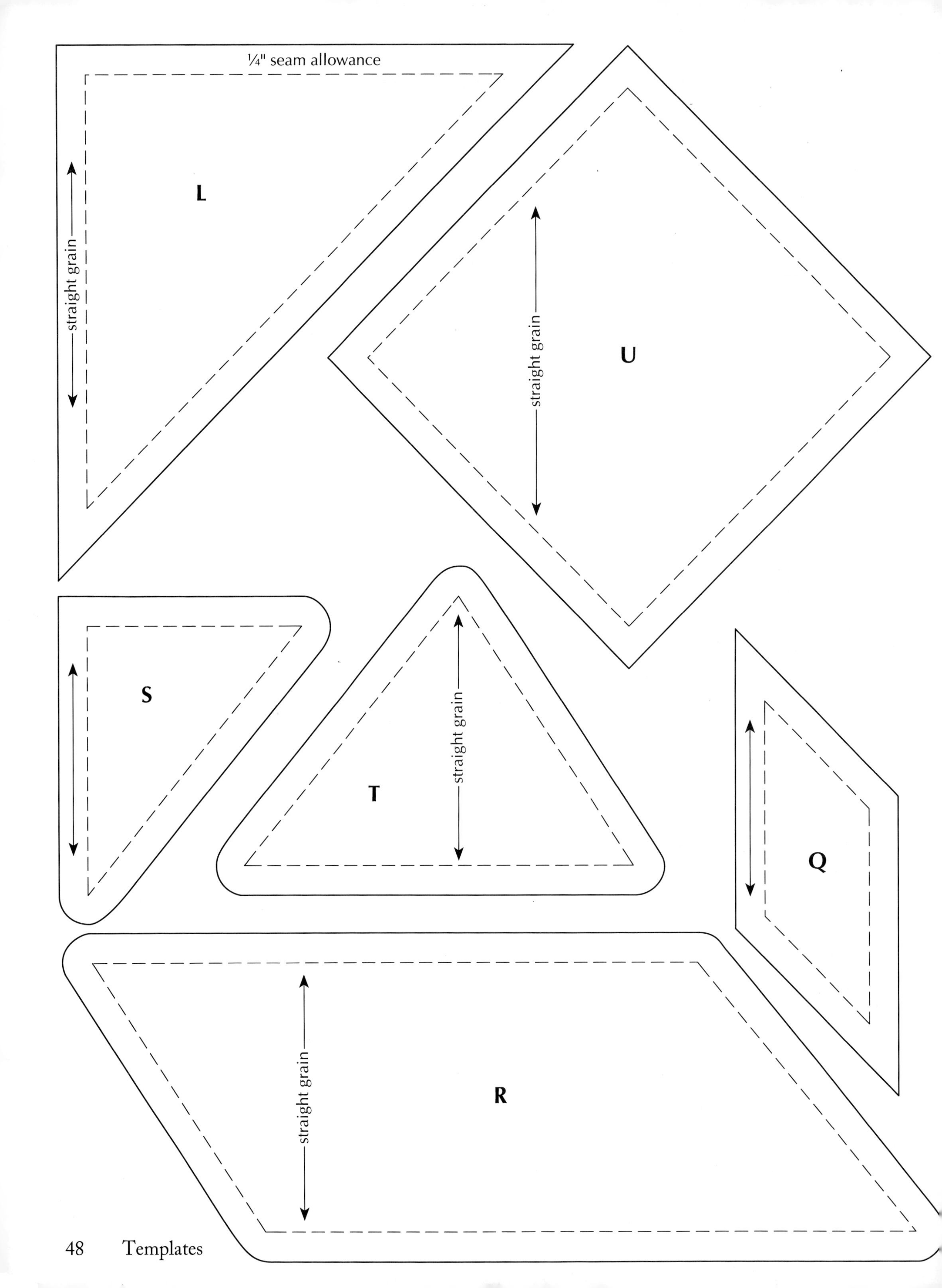
¼" seam allowance
L
straight grain
U
straight grain
S
T
straight grain
Q
R
straight grain